TWO PATHS

DISCOVER THE WAY THAT LEADS TO LIFE

CRAIG W. DOUGLAS

TWO PATHS: DISCOVER THE WAY THAT LEADS TO LIFE
Copyright © 2023 by Craig W. Douglas

All Scripture quotations, unless otherwise indicated, are taken from The Holy Bible, English Standard Version. ESV® Text Edition: 2016. Copyright © 2001 by Crossway Bibles, a publishing ministry of Good News Publishers. Used by permission. • Scripture quotations marked (NIV) are taken from Holy Bible, New International Version®, NIV® Copyright ©1973, 1978, 1984, 2011 by Biblica, Inc.® Used by permission. All rights reserved worldwide. • Scripture quotations marked (NLT) are taken from Holy Bible, New Living Translation, copyright © 1996, 2004, 2015 by Tyndale House Foundation. Used by permission of Tyndale House Publishers, Inc., Carol Stream, Illinois 60188. All rights reserved.

ISBN: 978-1-4866-2445-4
eBook ISBN: 978-1-4866-2446-1

Word Alive Press
119 De Baets Street Winnipeg, MB R2J 3R9
www.wordalivepress.ca

WORD ALIVE
—PRESS—

Cataloguing in Publication information can be obtained from Library and Archives Canada.

With humor, authenticity, and clarity, Craig Douglas pulls from personal stories and Bible narrative to hammer home a clear invitation for a confused generation with no direction.

—Jonathan Headley, Lead Pastor, Jubilee Church

Two Paths presents truth in a practical, authentic, and engaging way, highlighted by personal examples lived out through adventure and disarming honesty. I wish I'd had this book to read when I was a young man.

—Del Riemer, Pastor, Teacher, Outdoorsman

Two Paths is a straightforward, easy to follow road map for anyone needing clarity on how to live life well. Craig's vulnerability in his personal stories makes the book enjoyable and solidifies his message.

—Maureen Floris, Youth Worker, Youth Unlimited

Two Paths is a clearly written, practical, and enjoyable guide to help teens and young adults understand what a life submitted to Christ looks like.

—Rachael Jones, Youth Worker & Law Student

If you're looking for a very readable book that combines personal experiences, stories, and solid biblical content focussed on choosing a path that honors Jesus, then I'd encourage you to read this book.

—Dr. David Horita, Regional Director, Fellowship Pacific

This practical guidebook links biblical truths with clear invitations that challenge readers to ponder life choices wisely.

—M. Drury, M.N., Educator, Academic Editor

I believe *Two Paths* will be used by God to help many avoid being stalled at the start of the spiritual journey and instead grow to become lifelong followers of Jesus.

—Dick Reeve, Retired Pastor and Jail Chaplain

Two Paths lays out a discipleship journey that affirms biblical truth with engaging narrative storytelling and practical ideas especially relevant to young (and not-so-young) people today.

—David Edgerton, Rector and Lead Pastor, St. George Maple Ridge

This book is a great resource, as it teaches, challenges, and encourages people to take the narrow path that leads to life in Jesus. Though aimed at late teens and young adults, it contains relatable examples and truths that are beneficial to people of any age. I especially enjoyed the humor and choose-you-own-adventure-style summaries at the end of each chapter.

—Birgitta Westlund, Technical Communicator

Craig's witty stories, interspersed with straightforward and thoughtful advice from a biblical perspective, are engaging and will help readers avoid disaster and find the love of Jesus in everyday life. An excellent, concise book for teens or young adults, and also anyone looking to walk "the road less traveled by" or help others to do the same.

—Tim Larson, Outdoor Education Director, Camp Squeah

Two Paths is a helpful guide and a good discipleship primer for youth desiring to understand the nature of the Christian path and follow Jesus along it.

—Ron Redekop, Senior Pastor, Richmond Alliance Church

Two Paths belongs in the hands of young leaders because it uses accessible language with a storyteller's approach—without compromising really important, life-impacting principles.

—Darren Duncalfe, Executive Director, Charis Camp
and Conference Centre

For…
My adult children, Ben and Lorelle, and all the other leaders I have been privileged to teach. You constantly inspire me. May these words inspire you to follow Jesus with all your hearts, minds, souls, and strength.

Contents

Acknowledgments

Thank you to my wife, Leanne, for being a cheerleader and help throughout this long process. I never would have completed it if you hadn't believed in me.

Thank you to Marj Drury for all your sage advice and encouragement. You helped me believe that this project was worth doing.

Thank you to the Timberline Ranch board and staff for being understanding when I was less present than usual as I completed some of these tasks.

Thank you to all my Alpha and Beta readers, including Ben Douglas, Rebekah Jonker, Olivia Reid, Jim Badke, Kim Blackaby, Delayne Plesko, Dick Reeve, Del Riemer, Darren Duncalfe, Maureen Floris, Birgitta Westlund, Rachael Jones, Greg Shellborn, Kyle Reddemann, Tim Larson, Rob Tiessen, Greg Dalman, Jonathan Headley, Ron Redekop, David Horita, and David Edgerton.

Thank you to Word Alive Press for believing in this project and guiding me through the latter stages.

Thank you to my Lord and Savior, Jesus Christ, for bringing me through the many paths that have formed me and for providing the hope that has led to this book. Soli Deo Gloria!

Introduction
THE JOURNEY AHEAD

Make me to know your ways, O Lord;
teach me your paths.
~Psalm 25:4

Somehow, I took the wrong path and ended up far from where I wanted to go.

It was a beautiful spring day, and our family was visiting my mother in Victoria, British Columbia, Canada. My teenage daughter, Lorelle, and I decided to spend the afternoon hiking up Mount Finlayson, a relatively short but steep hike with a gorgeous view of the Olympic Mountains across the Strait of Juan de Fuca.

Lorelle is always game for exercise and adventure and was happy to leave the planning details to me—and the carrying of our pack with the water bottles and snacks. We drove to Goldstream Park and started up the trail among towering Douglas firs. I had to stop several times to take photos—a compulsion of mine. The path started out steep and then got steeper, but after about an hour of scrambling over roots and rocks, we made it to the top, took some great photos, and enjoyed a less-than-healthy cookie snack.

Before leaving home, I had checked an online map and had seen a loop we could take around the back of the mountain on the way down. It was somewhat longer, but it looked interesting, so I suggested we go that way. Lorelle liked the idea, and we began our descent. Counting on my good sense of direction, I knew that staying to the right would provide a clockwise route around the mountain and back to where we'd parked.

Unfortunately, we kept coming to trails I thought we should take, and they were blocked off and marked "closed"—I assume for repair. I had no paper map with me, but I trusted my instincts to find the way back. However, it wasn't long until I realized that my strategy of staying to the right was not working. We seemed to be walking in the wrong direction.

Eventually, the trail unexpectedly came out on a road, and I had no idea where we were. So I belatedly decided to check a map app on my phone. Sure enough, we had gone far out of our way. As the crow flies, we were literally about twice as far from the car as we had been on the summit! Fortunately, using my phone map, we were able to find our way along the roads back to Goldstream Park. However, my misdirection cost us almost an extra hour of hiking—on what should have been less than a two-hour hike!

CROSSROADS

I still don't know exactly where I went wrong on that hike. I've since looked over the maps, and I have some theories. All I know is that I must have taken a wrong turn somewhere. I stood at a crossroads, a fork in the trail, and chose poorly.

I love hiking, and I'm so blessed to live in a part of the world where hiking trails abound. There are hundreds of great trails within an hour of where I've lived for the past eighteen years in Maple Ridge, British Columbia. Yet in my adventures, I have discovered that not all paths are equal. Some lead to wondrous vistas and views, interesting rock formations, beautiful waterfalls, and incredible scenery. Others are much less interesting, and some are even quite dangerous. Certain paths start out looking promising, but they slowly dwindle to nothing or take you farther from your desired destination.

It's so easy to go the wrong way! I've often taken wrong or useless paths, only to retrace my steps. Other times, I've followed a trail that reviewers enjoyed, only to be disappointed. Sometimes my chosen routes have taken me into difficult circumstances, and occasionally, they have led me into unexpected danger.

Life's decisions are a lot like choosing a trail. There are options all around us as to where we will go and how we will spend these few precious years on this planet. The challenge is knowing where to go and what to do with that time.

THE HEART BEHIND THE BOOK

My children were teenagers when I began writing this book five years ago. I began writing specifically to them, chapter after chapter of lessons I had learned from life and God's Word. It was meant to be a legacy for them, a way of leaving something behind that they would perhaps read and consider as they faced many challenges ahead of them. As my family read some of the chapters, they urged me to complete the project and publish it for others to read.

After about a year of writing—and far too many words—I began to agree in my heart that what I had written for my family could be helpful for others if it was reduced and given better focus. Over the years, I've taught and mentored hundreds of young people, and as I rewrote the book, they were always in mind. I kept asking myself what I could possibly give them to help them on their way. I realized that the best I could offer was to direct them to Jesus through what he had taught me, especially in his Word.

So as you read this book, you'll likely hear a father's heart in it, the voice of someone who wants the best for his kids and this rising generation. As I grow older, I desperately desire for the ones who will replace me to know Jesus and follow him with all their hearts.

As much as this book was written with teens and younger adults in mind, it will benefit anyone who wants to follow Jesus—or who even wants to *want* to follow Jesus!—and is struggling along the path. It's written to be a guidepost, a sign pointing to God's wisdom.

> BONUS TIP: Along the way, you'll see some bonus tips like this. These are somewhat related thoughts— important to me or just humorous—that I insert to break up the narrative and hopefully encourage you to stop and consider.

FINDING GUIDANCE

Once, when camping, I found my way to an outhouse in the middle of the night. The sky was overcast, the area heavily treed, and it was pitch black, so I relied on my flashlight to see the path. I must have gotten turned around on the way back from the outhouse, and I started down a trail that didn't lead back to my tent. I experienced momentary panic as I realized I had no idea which direction to go to get back on track.

Even with my little flashlight, I could barely see the trail and didn't know where it would lead. Fortunately, even in my sleepy state, I was sensible enough to turn around and head back to the outhouse. I then tried to remember what angle I had walked to it from my tent, and I eventually found my way back safely. I must admit, however, that it was somewhat disconcerting and even a little frightening. I would have been in a difficult situation had my flashlight lost power.

I'm so glad God doesn't leave us to fend for ourselves in the dark. He hasn't simply given us life and breath and said, "Okay, people, now you go figure it out. Good luck!" Instead, he has given us wisdom from his *Word*, his *Spirit*, and his *people* to guide us. We don't have to guess where to go or how to live. We can know his will and the paths he wants us to take.

God's Word in Proverbs tells us, "*Ponder the path of your feet; then all your ways will be sure*" (Proverbs 4:26). Ponder. Consider. *Think* about the path you're on and where it's taking you. Wisely decide where to go. Proverbs also says, "*There is a way that seems right to a man, but its end is the way to death*" (Proverbs 14:12).

The alternative to thoughtfully and wisely choosing our steps is to carelessly go wherever seems or *feels* good and right. That's a path that leads to death! We have but one life to live. That's it! Then we enter eternity. Not only is our destiny at stake, but the quality and meaning of our lives. It can so easily be wasted if we choose unwisely.

The following chapters will take us on a journey through scripture and real-life experiences to illustrate the way of wisdom and how to make choices that will result in a full, productive, and meaningful life. I pray that God's Spirit will use this book to help guide you in his ways.

— Chapter One —

CHOOSING YOUR PATH

You make known to me the path of life;
in your presence there is fullness of joy;
at your right hand are pleasures forevermore.
~ Psalm 16:11

We always have a choice, but all choices are not equal. Some will bring you success, while others will bring you to ruin.

I used to enjoy reading *Choose Your Own Adventure* books. Each page was a short narrative followed by a choice. Do I pursue the dragon, or help the maiden in distress? Which town should I travel to? Do I drink the potion or not? Instead of reading about someone else's adventure, it made *me* the central character.

Each time I made a choice, the book would send me to a different page to continue the narrative and show me the results of my choice. Usually it allowed me to continue my adventure, but sometimes my choice would end in disaster. My character might die from drinking the potion, or I may not achieve my goal because I foolishly chased the dragon when I was supposed to save the maiden.

The great thing was that when I failed, I could either start over or simply go back to the previous page and make a different choice. My choices had no real consequences. In fact, it was sometimes fun to make an obviously poor choice and see what happened to my character!

LIFE IS ABOUT CHOICES

Fortunately, life's not like that. We don't have to make life-or-death decisions every few minutes, nor do we usually have to make essential decisions without any knowledge or context. However, most of the decisions we make have real-life consequences. We can never turn back the pages and change our choices. Right now, as I type, I'm choosing to keep writing instead of doing what I feel like doing—going outside and enjoying the sunshine! Five minutes from now, I may have to make that same choice, or I may have to choose whether to answer a text or ignore it for now.

Where I am right now is also the result of countless decisions I've made previously in my life. I can't easily change where I am today or what kind of person I am right now. However, tomorrow is unwritten, and the choices I make over the next twenty-four hours will, in many ways, determine where my life is at tomorrow.

Each day is also affected by many things beyond my control. Last week, I did all the cooking and cleaning because my wife was sick. There's not much I could have done about that, but I still had the choice of how to deal with it. For example, I could have been grumpy, or I could have embraced it as an opportunity to serve my wife. Even *that* choice was affected by previous decisions, for if I'd chosen resentment in the past, it would be much harder to choose grace in this situation.

Every choice takes us in a direction, and the sum of our choices creates the path of our life.

KNOW BEFORE YOU GO

I generally plan ahead when hiking, especially in a new area. Today we're fortunate to have many maps and tools on the internet to help us see paths before we start down them. I have an app that enables me to know the length of a trail, how long an average hiker takes to complete it, how much elevation gain and loss is involved, and how difficult others have rated it. It provides recent photos and even up-to-date trail conditions.

Similarly, we can "check out the trail ahead of us" in life before going there. Before we make a choice that takes us down any path in life, we can stop, determine what's ahead, and decide what to do, based on that information.

The trouble is that most of us live by *instinct* instead of wisdom. We often look ahead and make choices based on what *feels* right or *looks* good. I did that on our Mount Finlayson hike. Our culture fuels this by cultivating the lie that we need to "be true to ourselves" or "live our own truth." Somehow, we have become convinced that we're each smart enough and experienced enough to do what is best without any advice or help from anyone else.

> BONUS TIP: There is no such thing as a person's "own truth." A person's "own opinion" or "own feelings" about a situation are valid, but truth is not subjective. Believing something does not make it true for you or anyone else.

FOOLISHNESS

There's a word in the Bible used to describe this arrogance of assuming we always know the right paths to take: "foolishness." This is especially displayed in the book of Proverbs. A good summary of this is found in Proverbs 12:15: "*The way of a fool is right in his own eyes, but a wise man listens to advice.*" The "*way* of a fool is right in his own eyes" (emphasis added). In other words, the *direction* of a foolish person's life seems good to them. What they do *feels* right, and no one can tell them differently. In comparison to the wise person, this verse implies that a fool doesn't listen to advice. That's a major difference between wisdom and foolishness—whether we have the humility or not to admit that we don't have all the answers.

It's foolish to live by instinct, by feeling, hoping that we will somehow "get it right." It's like walking barefoot through a dark house with the power out and with toys all over the floor, hoping we don't step on them. You may get lucky for a while, but sooner or later, you'll step on that little piece of Lego, and it will hurt! Why not first grab a flashlight to see where you're walking?

The wise person brings light to each situation to find a path that avoids harm. The fool walks in the dark, assuming they know the way and can avoid dangers. We would call a person a fool who could have grabbed a flashlight and chose not to. Yet our society often celebrates those who make their own way in the world without listening to advice from others.

When children are young, we never assume they know the right thing to do. One day when my son was little, we were walking in a parking lot, and he suddenly pulled away and ran towards traffic on a busy road. It was terrifying! After I grabbed him, I had to sit him down and help him understand that he must *never* do that again. He was young, and he couldn't comprehend the danger around him. However, he listened to wisdom and thankfully never ran towards traffic again. *"A fool spurns a parent's discipline, but whoever heeds correction shows prudence"* (Proverbs 15:5, NIV).

The fool doesn't listen to those older and more experienced in life, whereas those with *prudence*—another word for *wisdom*—change their path when corrected. Accepting correction is not easy! As a young boy, I fought against it tooth and nail. I hated to be told what to do, and I often had to be disciplined for my behavior. I had a wild and foolish streak that needed to be corrected or I would have gone down many destructive paths.

Look at what a few of the Proverbs say about foolishness:

- *"Whoever trusts in his own mind is a fool, but he who walks in wisdom will be delivered"* (Proverbs 28:26).
- *"A fool takes no pleasure in understanding, but only in expressing his opinion"* (Proverbs 18:2).
- *"Like a dog that returns to his vomit is a fool who repeats his folly"* (Proverbs 26:11).
- *"Folly is a joy to him who lacks sense, but a man of understanding walks straight ahead"* (Proverbs 15:21).
- *"A fool's lips walk into a fight, and his mouth invites a beating. A fool's mouth is his ruin, and his lips are a snare to his soul"* (Proverbs 18:6–7).
- *"Doing wrong is like a joke to a fool, but wisdom is pleasure to a man of understanding"* (Proverbs 10:23).
- *"The fear of the Lord is the beginning of knowledge; fools despise wisdom and instruction"* (Proverbs 1:7).

Those who ignore wisdom—fools—could be summarized as follows:

- They trust what they think they know instead of listening to good advice.
- They love to hear themselves talk rather than listen to what others have learned.
- They don't learn from their own mistakes.
- They enjoy being foolish and taking crooked paths.
- They repeatedly say things they shouldn't, leading to much trouble.
- They find it funny to do and say what is morally wrong.
- They hate it when people correct them or try to show them better ways to live.

Reread these definitions and ask yourself, "Could I ever be considered a fool? Do the people I spend time with live these ways?"

WISDOM OR CONSEQUENCES?

We need wisdom to avoid dangerous, destructive, and useless paths. If you talk to people caught up in drug habits or crime, they often say they wish they'd listened to those who warned them not to go that way. They wish they could go back and make different choices, that they'd had the ability or the guts to say "no" to certain things along the way. Often they were influenced by friends or by those who didn't care about them or have their best interests at heart. They often wish a parent had set boundaries for them.

We always have options for which path we choose, and our choices are usually based on what we think will benefit us the most. Sometimes we recognize an unfruitful or harmful path because we've gone down it before and suffered for it. We can learn from those past consequences and make better choices next time.

Yet imagine if you had to learn *everything* that way! What if you had to learn the danger of walking too close to a cliff—by trial and error? Or what if you could never know that speeding was dangerous until you had a high-speed car crash? Or imagine if we could never know what plants were poisonous until we ate them? Yikes! We can't possibly learn *everything* by consequences, because some are deadly, others are crippling, and no one has enough time to learn everything that way, though some are determined to try.

The majority of what we know isn't something we've experienced ourselves. Instead, it's learned from trusted sources such as parents, teachers, some internet sites, and books. Fortunately, we can learn by listening to others who know better than us, paying attention to signs at the edge of cliffs, reading about which foods are safe to eat, etc. When I need to change a headlight on my car, I don't guess how to access it or what kind of bulb to use. I look in the manual. With trickier repairs, I can often find a YouTube video to help me, made by someone who has done it successfully.

It's much better to learn by *wisdom* than by consequences.

THE FOOLISH KING

Once upon a time, a young prince named Bo was in line to become king after his father. Bo watched his dad rule and believed he could do a much better job. Over the years, he saw his father make more and more erratic decisions, and he could hardly wait for the day to take over the throne.

Unfortunately, Bo was not a particularly good student, so he didn't pay attention during Monarch School and often skipped classes to party with his friends. Bo was very popular because he always had lots of money—and everyone knew they should treat the future king well.

When Bo's dad finally passed away, Bo was crowned king. All his friends congratulated him, and the good times began. Except for one problem: being a king meant Bo had to make many decisions that affected thousands of people. This was hard work! Bo suddenly realized he should have paid attention in class. Maybe he should have even chatted with his dad and learned a thing or two. Unfortunately, that opportunity was gone.

> BONUS TIP: When you know what you want to do with your life, do everything you can to become the absolute best you can be at that. Never settle for mediocrity in anything you do.

Things went well for a short time, but soon the people started pestering him to reduce the colossal taxation burden his dad had forced upon them. Bo wished they would just leave him alone. This was not how he thought it would be as king.

Bo realized he needed some advice, so he asked his father's old advisors what he should do. These older men had watched the events over many years and knew the people's hearts, so they advised Bo to reduce the taxation load. They were confident that the people would love and faithfully serve him if he did.

Bo considered this, but he realized that fewer taxes meant less money to enjoy, so he asked his buddies what they thought. They said, "More ale! Cheaper ale! More taxes so you can buy us more ale!" They told Bo it would be better to rule the people with an iron fist and *increase* the tax burden. After considering this briefly, Bo agreed that more money in the treasury would be better. He didn't want to disappoint his friends; besides, their advice lined up with what he wanted.

As you can guess, the story doesn't end well. Bo, also known as Rehoboam, was a real king who ruled the twelve tribes of Israel many years ago (see in the Bible, 1 Kings 11–12). He ignored wise advice and made a foolish decision. As a result, the ten northern tribes refused to submit to his rule and found a new king. The kingdom was divided, and only the two southern tribes, Judah and Benjamin, stayed faithful to Rehoboam.

During Rehoboam's reign, he allowed evil foolishness to flourish in his kingdom. God, therefore, allowed them to be conquered by Egypt for a time. There were also wars between the southern and northern tribes for hundreds of years, and the twelve tribes were never united again.

Understand this: *Rehoboam never got a second chance.* His one lousy choice held catastrophic consequences for everyone.

When we look at his upbringing, we see that his unwise decision was almost inevitable, given previous poor choices. His father Solomon's bad choices placed the kingdom in a precarious position. This ensured that Rehoboam's failure would be hugely amplified. God had given Solomon great wisdom, but he chose to ignore it in his later years, thus beginning the downward spiral of the kingdom.

Like Rehoboam, there are times when our choices have enormous consequences for our lives and the people around us.

GET WISDOM

Most people don't understand their crucial need for wisdom and discernment, especially in this information—and misinformation—age. Look at Proverbs 4:7–8: "*The beginning of wisdom is this: Get wisdom, and whatever you get, get insight. Prize her highly, and she will exalt you; she will honor you if you embrace her.*" The very beginning of becoming wise is to realize that you need wisdom! "*Get wisdom … get insight. Prize her highly …*" So where do we find wisdom?

Not long ago, my wife, Leanne, and I decided to kayak on Pitt Lake, just a twenty-minute drive from where we live, yet new for us. I had heard from others that there was a lovely river and campground accessible on the other side of the lake. I quickly looked at a map, and it seemed straightforward: cross the lake and paddle up the stream to the campground. However, after we crossed the lake, I couldn't see any river opening. We turned north and traveled along the shore until we found the mouth of a creek, but it didn't go anywhere and quickly became too shallow. So we turned south and eventually found the river behind a little island I had overlooked on the map. By this time, it was getting late, so we paddled back across the lake and went home.

> BONUS TIP: Hoping for the best should never be called a plan.

You can be sure the next time we went to Pitt Lake—on a beautiful, sunny day in October—I was much more prepared! I studied a map carefully, noted a better angle to cross the lake, and ensured I knew how far it was up to the campground. As expected, we easily found the river opening and proceeded up the river.

At one point, we could choose between two river channels that looked relatively equal in depth and width. I suddenly wished I had a map with me, but fortunately, as we got closer, we saw a sign pointing to the left for the campground. So helpful!

We continued up the river, laughing and having a great time. However, it was still quite far, and I wondered if we should turn back soon. Just as I was about to give up and turn around, two guys in a canoe came around a bend towards us, so I asked them how far to the campsite. "Like, two hundred meters," they said, "just around that bend." Great! So we paddled a little further, found the campsite, had a nice little break wandering around, took a few photos, ate a snack, and headed back.

What did it take for us to get to the campsite? A map, a sign, and a couple of friendly canoers. Then it just took some effort paddling. Similarly, we find wisdom through the *maps, signs,* and *people* God provides for us. His Word is like a *map,* his Spirit in us is like a *sign,* and his *people*—the community of believers—are also there to help us, encourage us, and keep us headed in the right direction. Wisdom comes from him.

1. God's Word

Looking at the very beginning of Proverbs, we see that it was written to help guide people into wisdom. The first four verses read:

> *The proverbs of Solomon, son of David, king of Israel:*
> *To know wisdom and instruction,*
> *to understand words of insight,*
> *to receive instruction in wise dealing,*
> *in righteousness, justice, and equity;*
> *to give prudence to the simple,*
> *knowledge and discretion to the youth—*

Not only was Proverbs written to help guide us to wisdom and truth, but the entire scriptures exist so that we can read them, understand them, and live by their principles. Psalm 119:105 says, *"Your word is a lamp to my feet and a light to my path."* God's Word is like that flashlight in your pitch-black house. It brings light to your path to clearly see where to go and to avoid those sharp toys scattered over the floor. It's like that flashlight I used to return to the campsite.

But a flashlight is only suitable for its intended purpose: to light your way. It makes a terrible hammer, and it's not a great ornament. You need to pick it up, turn it on, and point it where you want to go. Similarly, though some people use the Bible to "hammer" their opinions on others, and others leave it as an "ornament" on a bookshelf (see what I did there?), it's only beneficial when we pick it up, study it, and live by what it says.

You can disagree with what a flashlight reveals if you want. You can deny the existence of that pile of Lego it illuminates in the middle of your path. But if you don't heed what it clearly shows, you're in for some hurt! Similarly, we ignore the clear commands of scripture to our own peril.

> BONUS TIP: One great way to become wise is to meditate regularly on the book of Proverbs. There are thirty-one chapters, so some read one chapter daily, month after month.

2. God's Spirit

The Holy Spirit is often called the "Spirit of Wisdom" in the Bible (e.g., Ephesians 1:17). Amazingly, he lives inside all believers! He often nudges us in the right direction through our consciences (and sometimes even more directly), like a sign keeping us from getting lost along the way.

There's a fascinating narrative in Acts 16 that speaks of the Apostle Paul on one of his missionary journeys. It says in verse 7, "… *they attempted to go into Bithynia, but the Spirit of Jesus did not allow them.*" How strange! They discovered why they were held back when God sent Paul a vision of a man begging him to "*Come over to Macedonia and help us*" (v. 9). Verse 10 reads, "*And when Paul had seen the vision, immediately we sought to go on into Macedonia, concluding that God had called us to preach the gospel to them.*"

Sometimes God's Spirit speaks to our spirits, and we know we should go somewhere or stop and help someone or talk to them about Jesus. We may not get visions but subtler inward pushes and pulls.

> **BONUS TIP:** We should never refer to the Holy Spirit as "It." He is *God*, a member of the Trinity: Father, Son, and Holy Spirit. A Person, not a power.

However, God's Spirit never contradicts his Word, so we must prioritize what we know from the Word over what we "think we might feel." When we're still unsure, God also gives us people to help us understand which way to go.

3. God's People

God reveals his wisdom and will to us through others who follow him. Proverbs 1 continues in verse 8 with, "*Hear, my son, your father's instruction, and forsake not your mother's teaching ...*" God has given us wise parents, friends, pastors, and even Christian authors (hey?) who can help us know which paths to take. We need to listen to others who have experienced life and learned from following Jesus. Proverbs 13:20 says, "*Whoever walks with the wise becomes wise, but the companion of fools will suffer harm.*"

We learn a lot from others, so choose your companions carefully. However, wisdom from people should never take priority over God's Word or the leading of his Spirit. We all need to study the Bible for ourselves and not simply assume that what someone else tells us is accurate. There may be times when we need to stand alone on the Word of God and the witness of his Spirit.

Those guys in the canoe might have been lying or wrong, but their advice aligned with what I had previously seen on the map, so I had every reason to believe they knew what they were talking about. If we surround ourselves with people who have experience in the Christian life, those who know Jesus and the Word of God, and if we listen to them, they will often be able to help us find our way and avoid most of the dangers we face.

Wisdom should be pursued in God's Word, his Spirit, and his people. As we pay attention to these, God will show us which way to go. Then we just need to keep paddling!

MOTORCYCLE TRIP

One of the most foolish things I've done was choosing to ride my motorcycle to college, riding 1,500 kilometers in just over a day. I had just finished an exhausting summer at camp, and I needed to get to school in thirty hours.

I was young and strong, so how hard could it be? I calculated that I only had to average about fifty kilometers per hour to get there on time, so I could travel at about one hundred kilometers an hour and have plenty of time for breaks. I would drink lots of coffee, which would carry me through the night, and hey, I had ridden a few hundred kilometers before, so what was 1,500?

It was a grueling trip, and it could have killed me. I rode through the mountains in the middle of the night, and I was so cold that I tailed closely behind a semi-truck for a windbreak. By the time I found an open coffee shop at about 5:30 a.m., I was shivering and shaking so much that I could barely even hold my coffee or take a sip. A few hours of riding later, I was so sleepy that I had to pull over to the side of the highway and lie down for an hour or so while the trucks thundered past me. Not wise!

BONUS TIP: Don't do that.

I finally made it to college and to a meeting I was required to attend—on time. What an accomplishment … at the risk of my life! That night as I slept in my dorm room, I hit my head on the side of my desk without even waking up. When I finally awoke the next day, I had a nasty cut beside my eye and blood on my pillow. It probably served me right.

KNOWLEDGE IS NOT WISDOM

There is a vast difference between *knowledge* and *wisdom*. Sometimes knowledge and wisdom are used interchangeably, but there are two different concepts here we need to distinguish.

Knowledge means to obtain information, which is easy to do. I can find out almost anything I need or want to know in a few seconds online.

If I wonder about an actor in a movie I'm watching, before the scene even changes I can pull out my phone and find out his name, what other roles he's been in, his birthdate, where he grew up, and much more.

Wisdom, however, goes beyond knowledge. It's the proper or sound *application* of information. It means seeing two or more paths, understanding where each leads, and choosing the one that will take you where you *should* go. It's making the best decisions based on the information you have and getting more information if you need it.

Knowledge understands the force of gravity and how falling a great distance can injure or kill a person. It acknowledges fences along a cliff and signs warning about the danger of getting too close to the edge. But that knowledge only helps a person if they are wise enough to *heed* the warnings and stay on the safe side of the fence. A person can be very knowledgeable yet still very foolish.

I knew how to ride a motorcycle, how far I needed to go, and the speed I needed to average to make it to college on time. But it was foolish to try to get there in such a short time, especially given my exhaustion and inexperience traveling such a distance. I would have been wise to leave camp earlier or take a bus instead of riding my bike that far.

Unfortunately, wisdom is not highly sought-after in this world. When I was growing up, *prude* was an insult for someone who refused to follow the crowd when they were drinking, smoking, or otherwise acting foolishly. Interestingly, prude comes from *prudence*, another word for wisdom. Being wise has never been considered *cool*, and those who don't follow the crowd will usually be resented.

> BONUS TIP: If you seek to be wise, you'll stand out among your peers. They may resent you for it, but secretly they may respect you. Seeking approval from others is a terrible reason to be foolish.

Knowledge only takes us so far. Wisdom is essential as we chart a course for our lives and make daily decisions that affect our journey and ultimate destination.

ONE WAY

In John 13 and 14, Jesus begins to explain to his disciples that he would soon die and go back to the Father. Peter asks him where he is going, and Jesus simply tells him that where he is going, Peter can't come right now. But don't worry, Jesus tells them, because he will prepare a place for them and come back to get them!

Still not understanding, Thomas asks Jesus, "*Lord, we do not know where you are going. How can we know the way?*" (John 14:5). Jesus gives Thomas the now-famous answer: "*I am the way, and the truth, and the life. No one comes to the Father except through me*" (John 14:6). A little later, Jesus promises that he won't leave them alone but he will also give them the Holy Spirit to teach them and help them remember what Jesus taught them. So they did not need to worry or fear!

We need to understand that God *is* wisdom. His Spirit *is* wisdom. His Son, Jesus, also claimed to *be* wisdom incarnate by pointing to himself and saying, "*I am the way.*" He didn't just say he *knows* the way, but he *is* the way. He claimed that the only path to the Father in heaven is through him—by trusting in him and following him.

This is the essence of wisdom: deciding to follow Jesus instead of our own hearts and desires.

GRACE

Some days, trying to live for God threatens to overwhelm me. I look at others and know I can never be like them. I can never be good enough. I have to remember that the path leading to life is never about following a set of rules. Rather, it's about following a person, Jesus Christ, and having a relationship with him. This means no two paths will be alike, because Jesus doesn't lead us all on the same route. Your path in following Jesus will certainly have hills, valleys, successes, and setbacks different from mine. The destination is the same, but the routes are very different.

I think that's where grace comes in so beautifully. We can—and will—mess up along the way, but those detours become part of our unique path of following Jesus. It's easy to wrongfully see God as a taskmaster who is angry when we step off the path rather than as the gentle shepherd who knows that his sheep are prone to wander and willingly lays down his life to keep us safe. Not a day goes by without finding my feet wandering, but the grace and patience of a loving God bring me back again and again.

A LIFE-ALTERING CHOICE

When completing my master's degree at Northwest Baptist Seminary in 2005, I tried to discern God's will for my post-school life. I wanted to disciple people and teach them from the Bible, so I investigated many possibilities.

Leanne and I decided to take a day and go pray together at Cedar Springs, a camp just across the border. They graciously allowed us to use one of their A-frame buildings for the day, and we went to work—reading God's Word, walking, praying, and talking about what we were hearing from God.

> BONUS TIP: When you have to make a big decision, the wisest thing to do is take a break from all your thinking about it and spend considerable time seeking God.

It sounds so spiritual, but the day felt a bit like a disaster. Leanne had a headache all day, and we didn't feel like we were getting anywhere. However, we both left with a strong sense of *surrender* to God, that we were willing to go wherever he sent us, even if that meant leaving our home and moving to a small Bible school in the Prairies—something we had previously discussed and been opposed to.

As I continued to look for a teaching position, I stumbled upon a posting for a job as a camp director. Leanne hadn't grown up going to camp as I had, but she agreed that I should investigate it. One thing led to another, and we were invited to the camp to meet with the board. Soon after, I was asked to become their camp director.

There was only one problem. As we drove home from the meetings, neither of us had God's peace about taking the position. It seemed perfect on paper, but in our hearts, we felt God's Spirit saying, "No." I was very disappointed, but we knew we had to decline the position.

A year or so later, that camp closed for a few years due to some engineering issues, and the new director lost his job. Fortunately, God worked through that to take him and his wife to a better situation. We were so thankful we hadn't settled there and bought a house.

Meanwhile, because God had put camp work back on my heart, I wrote to one of the only other "camp people" I knew and asked if they knew of any other camps looking for a director. I had never emailed them before. Three weeks later, I received a return email saying, "We've just resigned as directors. May we pass your name on to the board?" It was interesting timing, to say the least, especially considering how long they had served there.

This was Timberline Ranch, a horse camp. They were looking for an interim director to serve for six months. My immediate response was, "No thanks!" I knew little about horses and was not looking for a temporary position requiring us to move, change schools for our son, and delay beginning my actual career. However, the board chairman "happened" to have met me at a youth retreat I'd hosted several years before. He contacted me personally, and I reluctantly agreed to meet with the board. Afterward, Leanne and I prayed about the position and agreed it made no sense, yet we came to believe that this was what God wanted us to do.

That was over eighteen years ago, and I'm still that camp's director! It's been very challenging at times, but I am confident that God directed us to this place and has sustained us throughout these years. Despite the hardships, I wouldn't trade it for anything, and I've learned to trust God more every year. Choosing God's wise leading doesn't mean he will lead us down easy paths. But now and eternally, the rewards are far beyond what we can imagine or hope for.

Follow wisdom; she will lead you on the right paths.

CHOOSE YOUR OWN ADVENTURE

The Wise Path: I choose to learn from God's Word, his Spirit, and godly people with much experience.

The Foolish Path: I choose to learn from consequences and hope for the best!

Discussion questions for each
chapter can be found at
cwdouglas.com under "Resources."

— Chapter Two —

BECOMING FIT FOR THE TREK

For while bodily training is of some value,
godliness is of value in every way,
as it holds promise for the present life
and also for the life to come.
~ 1 Timothy 4:8

Taking an easy path takes much less effort, but easy doesn't usually mean better.

I grew up playing many sports, especially soccer, and I was blessed with some natural abilities. However, I had to learn that ability doesn't bring success if it isn't combined with hard work.

When I was eleven, our physical education teacher suggested that some of us run the Victoria Half-Marathon with him. I was already playing soccer and doing track and field, so why not? I had no real idea how long twenty-one kilometers was, but if others were doing it, surely I could. So I signed up and ran. And ran. And walked ... As I met friends along the way, we jogged together for a while. Eventually, I crossed the finish line, just a few seconds over two hours. Not a world-class time, but I made it! I was utterly exhausted, and boy, was I ever sore for the next few days.

A year later, I ran the same race without stopping or walking and finished twenty-five minutes faster, placing me in the top ten for sixteen years and younger. Most importantly for me, this time I beat my P.E. teacher!

The difference? *Training.* I decided I wanted to do better and began training months before the event. I often gave up my lunchtimes at school to go to the track and run. Despite other kids sometimes jeering or trying to trip me as I trained—the little rotters—I persevered because I wanted to be in great shape for that race and others I was entering.

THOUGHTS AND HABITS

Becoming fit for life's trail means we must *train* ourselves to follow Jesus. That requires focus and effort.

It was probably a little foolish to attempt a half-marathon without proper training, but at least I was already in decent shape from all the other sports I enjoyed, including track. My usual routine included eating healthily, drinking sufficient water, getting lots of sleep, and being active much of the day—probably *too* active for some of my teachers. My baseline health was good even before I trained specifically for that race.

How fit are you for following Jesus? What is your *baseline*? In other words, without doing anything differently, how fit are you for this life journey? How can you even tell? Ralph Waldo Emerson wrote, "Sow a thought, and you reap an action; sow an act, and you reap a habit; sow a habit, and you reap a character; sow a character, and you reap a destiny."[1] There's a lot of truth to this. Our daily habits indicate where we will be in a year, five years, or even twenty years. How we think is how we live, and how we live is what we become.

Where do habits come from? They come from making the same choice day after day. They come from our *thoughts*—what we believe to be true about ourselves and our world. For example, if I want to become a great pianist, I need to choose to practice for several hours each day. However, to keep that up, I must honestly believe that I *can* become a great pianist, that I *want* to be a great pianist, and that it is *worth* doing all this hard work to achieve this goal. I'd also need to find a great teacher to wisely guide me towards my goal.

This is why I am not a great pianist—or great at any instrument. I don't *believe* I have the ability or drive to achieve that goal, and I don't *believe* pursuing it to that degree would be worthwhile.

> BONUS TIP: You don't have to become great at music,
> art, or sports to *enjoy* them. You'll often receive satisfaction

proportionate to the effort you put into it, but don't think
you need to be highly talented to find enjoyment.

Do you see that what we think about—what we believe—drives our habits, and our habits make us who we are? What we believe about ourselves and the world around us has everything to do with the paths we choose.

WORLDVIEW

Of course, if we're all mere accidents, evolutionary flukes with no meaning or purpose beyond what we can get out of this life, none of this matters. As the writer of Ecclesiastes says regarding life apart from God: "*So I recommend having fun, because there is nothing better for people in this world than to eat, drink, and enjoy life*" (Ecclesiastes 8:15a, NLT).

We all see people with this basic philosophy: do whatever makes you feel good and enables you to get the most out of life. Because they think this way, their habits follow. If they believe there is no God to judge their actions, they'll probably live without much accountability. If they believe exercise will make them feel or look better, and those things are important to them, they'll likely exercise. If they believe they need to keep their job to survive, they'll probably show up to work on time most days.

Our *actions* display our true beliefs. If I regularly sleep in on Sundays and miss church, I believe sleep is more important than church. If I only donate to the church when I have money left over after spending the rest on myself, I believe my needs or wants are more important than supporting God's ministries.

Our path, therefore, is determined by what we believe to be true about God, ourselves, and our surroundings. This is our *worldview*. A.W. Tozer, one of the foremost Christian thinkers of the twentieth century, wrote, "What comes into our minds when we think about God is the most important thing about us."[2] So what comes to mind when you think about God? Is he kind? Is he vindictive? Does he know or care about what's happening in our world? Where did you get your ideas about God?

Some of our understanding of our heavenly Father may come from our relationship with our earthly fathers. I always knew my dad loved me, though he rarely, if ever, said so, but he worked very hard to provide for our family and bring my sister and me up well. This meant strict discipline at times. Since I was prone to rebellion and disobedience, my parents spent a lot of effort correcting my behavior and attitudes. Spanking was acceptable in those days, and I was on the receiving end of many. I'm thankful they didn't allow me to go my own way.

> **BONUS TIP:** If or when you have children, consider that all good and proper discipline is an act of love and needs to be understood as such by the children. Loving them also means teaching them to avoid harmful habits and helping them develop beneficial habits.

My parents' rules seemed arbitrary and unfair at times. For example, I had to be home at least fifteen minutes before supper was served at 5:30. If I was five minutes late (i.e., 5:20), I knew I'd be in trouble. I wasn't allowed any candy except on Sundays and special occasions. We weren't allowed playing cards in the house. I even got in trouble for fistfights with other kids! I had unbelievably strict parents …

Once, when I was little, I struck a neighbor boy with a metal toy gun. My parents read me the riot act and grounded me, as I deserved. Later that evening, the boy came over to see if I could come out and play, but my mother told him, "No, he can't come to play because he hit you." I thought, *He's over it; he's forgiven me! Why can't I go play?* But my parents knew I would only learn if there were consequences.

Possibly because of my relatively strict upbringing and a strong emphasis on God's holiness at church, I grew up envisioning God as a disciplinarian. I imagined that he was never pleased with my behavior. I was saved and forgiven … but only until my next shenanigan.

I probably wanted God to be like my Uncle John, an older relative who never had children. To me, he embodied the spirit of Santa Claus. He had a full white beard, I saw him mainly at Christmas, he was very kind, and he always brought me wonderful, well-thought-out presents.

He rarely disciplined me, and I knew he loved me. If only God could be more like that!

Yet God is not what *we* make him or decide about him. Have you ever heard people say things like, "Well, *my* God would never allow children to suffer like that," or "*My* God would never condemn someone for just being themselves and following their natural desires"? People probably mean that *if* God exists, that being would act in ways consistent with how *they* think God should act. We often base our understanding of God on how we think *we* would act in his position. In other words, although God originally created people in his image, we go to great lengths to recreate him in ours.

A KNOWABLE GOD

Wouldn't it be helpful if God would somehow *tell* us about himself? Then we wouldn't have to base our understanding of him on our feelings or experiences with authority figures. After all, our beliefs guide our paths. As followers of Jesus, we believe that God has revealed himself. He has spoken to us in three distinct ways: the Written Word, the Living Word, and Creation.

The Bible is the *Written Word* of God. He spoke it to prophets, who wrote it down for us. Hebrews 1:1 says, "*Long ago, at many times and in many ways, God spoke to our fathers by the prophets ...*" This passage continues to say that Jesus is God's *Living Word*. He has shown us *precisely* what the Father is like.

> ... *but in these last days he has spoken to us by his Son, whom he appointed the heir of all things, through whom also he created the world. He is the radiance of the glory of God and the exact imprint of his nature, and he upholds the universe by the word of his power.* (Hebrews 1:2–3a; see also John 1:1–2)

God has also revealed himself to us through His *Creation*. Look at Psalm 19:1–4a:

The heavens declare the glory of God,
and the sky above proclaims his handiwork.
Day to day pours out speech,
and night to night reveals knowledge.
There is no speech, nor are there words,
whose voice is not heard.
Their voice goes out through all the earth,
and their words to the end of the world.

God wants us to know him, yet many resist him by suppressing the truth.

For the wrath of God is revealed from heaven against all *ungodliness and unrighteousness of men, who by their* *unrighteousness suppress the truth. For what can be known* *about God is plain to them, because* God has shown it to them. *For his invisible attributes, namely, his eternal* *power and divine nature, have been clearly perceived, ever* *since the creation of the world,* in the things that have been made. *So they are without excuse.* (Romans 1:18– 20, emphasis added)

We don't like to think about a holy, wrathful God because it's more comforting to think of him as loving. Yet he is both holy *and* loving— and much more. This passage tells us that God has plainly shown himself to *all* people. No one can claim they don't know that God exists. Creation itself—*"the things that have been made"*—makes it clear there is an eternal, all-powerful God.

This is the basis for wisdom. It's the basis for all the right paths in our lives—that we understand that God has revealed himself to us and desires a relationship with us.

CHRISTIAN ATHEISTS

For all God has done to show himself to us, many who claim to be Christians live like God doesn't exist. They use the title "Christian" without following what Jesus says. They may as well be atheists for how their so-called "belief" in him affects their day-to-day lives.

This should be unsurprising since, again, how we think is how we live. We ought to examine our lives to see if *what we say we believe* matches *how we live*. If my life revolves around pleasing myself, my actual beliefs probably have very little to do with the God of the Bible. It's hypocritical to live for myself and claim to serve God.

Interestingly, the word "hypocrite" comes from a Greek word meaning "actor," someone who puts on different masks for different scenes in a play. For one scene, they are an artist; for another, a beggar; and for another, a prince. Who are they, really? None of these! Just an actor playing different roles as needed.

I was a hypocrite in many ways as I grew up. I went to church on Sundays and lived as I pleased the rest of the time. I may not have done most of the bad things some kids did, but I certainly wasn't living for God. It wasn't until high school that God convinced me that following him was the best way to live—and it absolutely is!

> BONUS TIP: There's no need to be defensive when people say the church is full of hypocrites. It's true, and I'm often one of them. What I say I believe doesn't always line up with my thoughts or actions. The good news is that God has forgiven me and is still working in me.

I was fortunate to grow up with parents who loved Jesus and brought me up in a Bible-believing church where I learned about Jesus and what it meant to follow him. I first trusted in Jesus when I was very young. However, my fear of being different or mocked for being a Christian prevented me from talking about Jesus to my friends, and I was embarrassed when anyone discovered I went to church. My behaviors proved what I truly believed: following Jesus was embarrassing.

This began to change when I started attending our church youth group in grade nine. I met young men and women just a few years older than me who genuinely loved Jesus and were still "cool." One leader, Ken, played guitar and wrote some great songs that we sang, and his passion for Jesus was contagious. His brother Stan, a physics major in university, was hilarious and obviously loved Jesus. He would drive me home from youth group in his—I thought—very fancy Honda Accord, playing Christian pop music, which I had never heard before but eventually learned to enjoy.

Dave, our youth pastor in my later high school years, made me a leader in the youth group and allowed me to plan and run Friday night events. Sometimes I failed, and he helped me pick up the pieces. He led mid-week Bible studies and taught us to memorize important scripture passages, such as the entire chapter of Romans 12. He also encouraged us to read the Bible for ourselves daily and spend time in personal prayer. In my grade twelve year, he met with me weekly for breakfast. We made a deal that if either of us missed our daily quiet time with God that week, that person had to pay for breakfast. Since I was cheap and none-too-rich, that certainly encouraged me to develop good habits quickly!

These young men and women trained me for the trail ahead by intention and example. They helped me grow in my understanding of who God is by filling my mind with scriptures and songs that burst with truth. They helped me see that living for Jesus was normal and not just for "super-Christians." I saw them go through their own struggles and trust God amid them. I saw them exemplify solid habits of Bible study and prayer. Seeing others living out their faith made an immense impact on my life. I decided that I too wanted to live for Jesus, no matter what it cost me.

Perhaps a lack of solid Christian examples leads us to live like atheists or be hypocritical. Maybe we just haven't been taught better. Yet this problem persists: far too many who claim to be Christians consistently act like there is no God.

FOLLOWING JESUS

The solution to Christian atheism is simple, but it's not easy. It's *making the daily choice to follow Jesus*. He not only *knows* the way to go, but he *is* the Way, the Truth, and the Life (John 14:6).

Getting started on the journey with Jesus is as simple as putting our trust in him, believing that he died on the cross in our place to take the penalty for our sins and that he rose from the dead, bringing eternal life to all who believe. We are saved by God's grace, through faith, not by any works we could do to receive his favor (see John 3:16; Ephesians 2:8–9; Romans 6:23). Yet true faith, true belief, *always* results in actions in line with those beliefs (see James 2:14–26). Jesus said that following him—taking the path to true life—would never be easy.

> *Enter by the narrow gate. For the gate is wide and the way is easy that leads to destruction, and those who enter by it are many. For the gate is narrow and the way is hard that leads to life, and those who find it are few.* (Matthew 7:13–14)

The first step to following Jesus is simply choosing the narrow gate and road, the way of the cross.

> *Then Jesus told his disciples, "If anyone would come after me, let him deny himself and take up his cross and follow me. For whoever would save his life will lose it, but whoever loses his life for my sake will find it. For what will it profit a man if he gains the whole world and forfeits his soul? Or what shall a man give in return for his soul?"* (Mathew 16:24–26)

If we're going to get serious about following Jesus, it's not going to be a picnic. We have to deny ourselves, which means choosing—day after day—to do what *he* has called us to do, not simply what *we* want to do. When we truly understand and believe that he has called us to live for him, that will lead to healthy habits. But it starts in the mind with what we *believe*, not just what we *say* we believe.

THINK DIFFERENTLY

When I coached soccer, I found improving players' physical skills relatively straightforward and predictable. I used drills, physical fitness, and scrimmages to help them improve. Yet I often found that improving those skills didn't translate into better play during games. I had to find better ways to train their *minds* to make the right decisions so that their physical skills would be useful.

I also discovered that practice does not make *perfect*! If you practice the wrong things, you will inevitably do the wrong things when it comes time for the game. What practice does is gradually make something *permanent*. If you practice poorly, you'll play badly. Thus, we must ensure that our practices—our habits—are the paths we want our lives to take.

One of the most skilled players I ever coached was also one of the laziest. He often showed up late for practices, didn't work hard at the drills, and rarely seemed to listen to my coaching. One skill I taught my players was to practice placing the ball low into the corners on penalty kicks. These sixteen-year-olds played at the highest level for their age, and the goalkeepers were usually very tall. A shot low in the corner from twelve yards away would almost always elude them, even if not struck too hard. Also, if they aimed low, they would be much less likely to miss the net, since they would never shoot the ball *over* the goal.

Once in a tournament semi-final, the game ended tied, and we went to penalty kicks—five shots each to determine the winner. I chose the boys to take these and reminded them to hit it low to the corners. Our final shot came down to this young superstar. Score, and we win the game and go to the final. Miss, and the kicks continue in "sudden death." Unsurprisingly, this skilled young player ignored my coaching and pounded the ball hard and high, well over the goal. The other team scored on their next shot. One miss later, we were on our way home, eliminated from a tournament we could have won.

> BONUS TIP: Learn to listen—and listen to learn. Even those at the top of their sport or field need coaching and always have more to learn.

If we want to change how we *act*, we must train ourselves to *think* differently and practice what we learn to be true. We need to be purposeful in focusing our minds on wisdom. The antidote to foolish living, or being "conformed to this world," is to be *transformed* in our minds: *"Do not be conformed to this world, but be transformed by the renewal of your mind ..."* (Romans 12:2a).

In practical terms, this "renewal" means *focusing* on truth. Biblical meditation means studying, thinking about, and memorizing scripture so that it stays in our minds and trains our thinking throughout the day. This is opposite to Eastern meditation, which is the practice of *emptying* one's mind, and we must be careful to distinguish between the two. We want to *fill* our minds with truth so that we experience transformation.

When bankers train to recognize counterfeit money, they don't study 712 different types of counterfeit money. They don't need to. Besides, that would be so boring that no one would want the job. All they need to do is study, feel, and smell the *real thing* over and over and over again. They fill their minds and senses with what is *authentic*. Then it is immediately evident to them when any kind of fake money appears.

We become what we *think*. We are transformed by what regularly enters our minds. If we constantly dwell on negative thoughts, we will become negative people. If we constantly think about things that aren't true, that will influence how we act. This is why God's Word tells us:

> *... whatever is true, whatever is honorable, whatever is just, whatever is pure, whatever is lovely, whatever is commendable, if there is any excellence, if there is anything worthy of praise,* think about these things. *What you have learned and received and heard and seen in me—* practice these things, *and the God of peace will be with you.* (Philippians 4:8–9, emphasis added)

Consider the sources you accept as true. Much of what we read online and on social media is people's opinions, not facts. Sure, there are verifiable news stories, and these are relatively easy to fact-check. However, accepting whatever we read as true without carefully checking sources is pure laziness. So often people form opinions based on a *headline*, not the story!

BONUS TIP: Be skeptical but not cynical. Question things to find the truth but not to prove that nothing is trustworthy. It's too easy to develop an arrogant attitude that assumes everyone is gullible except you. Be that person who looks for solutions, not just someone who points out all the problems.

If I feed myself a regular diet of lies, conspiracy theories, alternative news sites, glamour magazines, messed-up song lyrics, and TV shows that glorify sin, guess what—I will believe almost *anything* because I have trained my mind to believe lies. But if I consistently focus on *truth* and fill my mind with the Word of God, then when something false comes along, I'll have an easier time identifying it and calling it out for what it is. This is called *discernment,* a form of wisdom by which we can tell whether something is morally right or wrong, good or bad.

Because lies abound, we constantly need to fill our minds with scripture. God told his people to keep his Word with them wherever they went:

> *And these words that I command you today shall* be on your heart. *You shall* teach them *diligently to your children, and shall* talk of them *when you sit in your house, and when you walk by the way, and when you lie down, and when you rise. You shall bind them as a sign on your hand, and they shall be as frontlets between your eyes. You shall* write them *on the doorposts of your house and on your gates.* (Deuteronomy 6:6–9, emphasis added)

ACT DIFFERENTLY

There is a cosmic battle raging for control over your mind. The enemy of your soul wants you to follow the broad path of foolishness that leads to destruction. Your loving heavenly Father wants you to follow the narrow path of truth and wisdom that leads to life.

When we consistently fill our minds with the right things, the right actions will naturally follow. Right thinking (orthodoxy) inevitably leads to right living (orthopraxy). When we think correctly, we can begin to form the habits or disciplines to keep us on the right path. What are these?

Much has been written and is said about the need for good physical habits, like getting enough sleep, eating nutritious food, keeping hydrated, and exercising regularly. It's easy to consider these as being non-spiritual, but understand that everything physical affects us mentally and spiritually. For instance, when I'm grouchy, sometimes the best thing I can do for my family and myself is to take a nap or get to bed earlier that night.

We are not the sum of unrelated parts but a whole. My discipline of eating well and getting exercise not only *affects* my spiritual walk with Jesus; it also *reflects* my walk with Jesus. The Bible has much to say about looking after our bodies—which are the temple of God!

I find it interesting that the Jews' Sabbath, the day set aside each week for worship and rest, started at sundown the night before. Could that be because proper worship starts the night before with a good rest? I'm a terrible worshiper when I'm sleepy! God established a *Sabbath rest* by his own example in creation, where he worked six days and then rested. Proper rest isn't just a good idea. It's a profoundly spiritual act.

Our mental practices are also deeply spiritual, especially how we fill our minds. Consider the effect of spending 99 percent or more of our free time filling our heads with what we see on social media, television, movies, video games, etc.

A HEALTHY RHYTHM

What we need is a healthy *rhythm* of following Jesus. When I play in a band, it's easy for us to slowly get out of sync. In other words, the singing or the instruments aren't entirely in rhythm. As I play guitar and sing, it's easy to unintentionally slow down for quieter parts of a song or speed up when it gets louder. The easiest way to fix that is to *listen* carefully to the drums—assuming your drummer can stay on beat!—or use a metronome. We'll be in rhythm if we listen and play to the same beat.

Our lives are like that as well. Unless we listen to the Holy Spirit, we tend to get out of sync with God and others following him. Disciplines help us stay in rhythm with God. They are daily reminders of why we're doing what we're doing—and for whom.

Take the age-old practice of saying grace or asking the blessing before a meal. We do this because Jesus gave us the example, a practice long before his earthly time. I used to think God would be mad at me if I forgot, so even in public school I would say a quick, silent prayer before eating my lunch, making sure no one noticed. However, this discipline is for *our* benefit, not God's. At least three times every day, we're invited to stop and remember who provides our food, shelter, and clothing. It becomes part of our natural rhythm of life.

Similarly, part of my daily rhythm is to study my Bible and spend some time in prayer before I have breakfast. It centers me upon Jesus every day at about the same time. It's not that God will "zap" me if I sleep in, or that I'll do more evil that one day I forget—it's primarily for *my* benefit. Leanne and I also read scripture and pray together at breakfast and then finish the day praying together. As I practice these disciplines—these rhythms—over time, they draw me closer to God and slowly transform me into the image of his Son.

Further on, we'll look at various *spiritual disciplines* that will help us stay fit for and on the trail. But of primary importance, as we set out on the trail, we need to ensure that we're in the habit of *training our minds to follow Jesus*, spending time in and with the Word of God.

How we *think* is how we *live*, and how we *live* is what we *become*. The trail we're following today reveals our eventual destiny. Make sure you're on the narrow path that leads to Life!

CHOOSE YOUR OWN ADVENTURE

The Wise Path: I choose to train and renew my mind daily with God's revealed truth.

The Foolish Path: I choose to fill my mind with things that convince me that life is all about me and that I'm better on my own.

— Chapter Three —

TRAVELING LIGHT

For where your treasure is,
there your heart will be also.
~ Matthew 6:21

One summer, I decided to work at a secular camp instead of the Christian camp where I'd spent so many years. Camp Thunderbird was in the gorgeous foothills of Sooke, British Columbia, on Vancouver Island, and I was excited about the opportunity to learn and grow in a new camp environment.

Our staff training week included a backpacking trip into the wilderness. We'd be gone a couple of nights, so we packed everything we needed, including our personal items, tarps, groundsheets, food, utensils, and sleeping bags. Each of our packs weighed over fifty pounds.

After hiking for several hours, we finally reached our campsite, and I was exhausted. We all put our packs down, and then one of the guys, Jim, started giggling. We all wondered what (else) was wrong with him when he exclaimed, "Hey, Travis, take a look in your pack!"

As Travis began to open his pack, Jim laughingly explained what he had done. Back at the camp, when Travis wasn't watching, he had inserted a massive rock into his pack. Boy, did Travis look upset! We laughed along with Jim, but then as Travis reached into his pack to find the rock, *he* began to laugh. I was glad to see Travis was such a good sport. But then he turned to Jim with a big grin, and I wondered what was happening.

"Maybe," Travis said with a big smile, "you should check *your* pack, Jim!"

Jim's big grin dropped as he opened his pack and reached in. Sure enough, a heavy rock was hidden in *his* gear! Travis explained that he'd found it in his bag before leaving, and he managed to sneak it into Jim's pack.

I knew it was going to be an interesting summer with these guys.

> **BONUS TIP:** "Do unto others as you would have them do unto you." Or perhaps, "Live by the sword, die by the sword." Or maybe even, "What goes around comes around." Basically, be careful what you do to others, because there may be consequences![3]

TRAVELING WITH A PURPOSE

Backpacking with unnecessary weight is, well, unnecessary! Therefore, many backpackers pay exorbitant sums for the latest and lightest new gear. Backpacks, stoves, sleeping bags, hiking shoes, and tents are all made with materials and metals that are incredibly light and strong. They buy freeze-dried food, which weighs practically nothing because the water has been removed. Even an extra pound or two makes a difference when hiking a trail for long distances. You need to pack carefully and wisely, only bringing what you genuinely need.

To travel light means to travel with *intention*, leaving behind whatever slows you down or distracts you from that purpose. We get a sense of this in Hebrews 12:1–2a:

> *Therefore, since we are surrounded by so great a cloud of witnesses,* let us also lay aside every weight, *and sin which clings so closely, and let us run with endurance the race that is set before us, looking to Jesus, the founder and perfecter of our faith* ... (emphasis added)

The writer of Hebrews provides a history of faithful believers and how they endured all sorts of hardships but never received their reward during their lifetimes. Often they died martyrs' deaths, faithfully holding to God's assurance that it was all worthwhile.

He then addresses current believers who want to follow Jesus faithfully, reminding us that we're not the first to tread this difficult path. A *"cloud of witnesses"* has gone ahead, leaving us with their faithful example. People like Abraham, Moses, Gideon, Barak, David, and all the prophets—they faced hardships and endured! Despite torture, hunger, stoning, and worse, they continued to press on in faith and hope.

Some were tortured and refused to deny their faith *"so that they might rise again to a better life"* (Hebrews 11:35). Why would anyone willingly go through such mistreatment? They valued their eventual reward above an easy path. Their purpose for living was to love and serve the God who created and sustained them.

Understanding this, we're encouraged to likewise live with such a purpose, to *"run with endurance the race that is set before us."* We need to stay on the narrow, difficult path. The writer gives us two ways to do this: *"lay aside every weight and sin"* and *"look to Jesus."* In other words, we must eliminate everything that stops us from following Jesus and focus on him.

These two concepts are connected: if our eyes are fully on Jesus, we *will* lay aside anything and everything that stops us from following him. The greatest command, Jesus said, is to love the Lord with all our heart, soul, and mind (Matthew 22:37). To love God is to give him everything we have in complete obedience (1 John 5:3). I don't think it's an overstatement to say that most Christians have never adequately been taught the purpose of life: to love God and bring him glory.

It's apparent that many Christians have been *saved* but never *discipled.* They're easily fooled by Satan's terrible lie that they can have Jesus as an add-on to their lives and then just live as they please before going to heaven.

> **BONUS TIP:** Jesus never made following him an optional part of being saved. Nor is it something only mature Christians do. Consider what it means to be saved and to live out what Jesus has done for you and put into you. See 2 Corinthians 13:5.

THE HINDRANCE OF STUFF

Christians living self-centered lives may be easier to find in wealthy locales than in places of poverty or persecution. If I look at my context in North America and the Western world in general, it's evident that many who attend Christian churches or call themselves Christians have lost the purpose for which they were created. Being a Christian is little more than a cultural identification, often deeply tied to their (seemingly much more important) political affiliation.

So many Christians are content to make lots of money to have nice houses, furniture, cars, boats, and vacations and then leave a good inheritance to their children. Is this not what Jesus warned about in Luke 12:15? *"And he said to them, 'Take care, and be on your guard against all covetousness, for one's life does not consist in the abundance of his possessions."*

To be clear, I'm not railing against the rich. God has blessed Leanne and me with *much* more than we need, and we live exceedingly privileged lives. The real issue isn't whether you have lots or little but where your *heart* is. Some poor people are covetous and spend much time thinking about their few possessions and how to get more. Some wealthy people can be generous and keep their hearts free from the love of money. Yet we can't have it both ways. We can't truly follow Jesus *and* love money more than him. Jesus said:

> *Do not lay up for yourselves treasures on earth, where moth and rust destroy and where thieves break in and steal, but lay up for yourselves treasures in heaven, where neither moth nor rust destroys and where thieves do not break in and steal. For where your treasure is, there your heart will be also ... No one can serve two masters, for either he will hate the one and love the other, or he will be devoted to the one and despise the other. You cannot serve God and money.* (Matthew 6:19–21, 24)

Our possessions can easily weigh us down and keep our hearts from following Jesus. When money or possessions become our focus, we will inevitably wander down paths that take us far from Jesus: *"For the love of money is a root of all kinds of evils. It is through this craving that some have wandered away from the faith and pierced themselves with many pangs"* (1 Timothy 6:10).

A few years ago, my board allowed me to take a sabbatical, and Leanne and I decided to take a once-in-a-lifetime trip to Europe with our teenage kids. We spent all of August and most of September traveling to England, Scotland, Italy, Switzerland, Germany, Austria, Greece, and a few other places.

I spent months planning our itinerary, as I wanted to make the most of our trip and keep it as inexpensive as possible. One of the big challenges was figuring out what to pack. We'd be driving most of the time, and cars in Europe tend to be small, so we wanted everything to fit in the trunk (or "boot") of the cars we rented. Eventually, we decided to purchase some small, squishable suitcases, and we were allowed to bring only what would fit into these and in a small backpack. That way, each person could throw their backpack on, grab their suitcase, and travel nimbly.

However, it was a challenge to pack so lightly! Traveling to the UK, we had to plan for inclement weather, but we'd also have hot weather in Greece. So we needed many types of clothing, since we wouldn't always be able to wash our clothes. Then there were electronics to include, books I wanted to read, and other items I thought I might need but wasn't sure about.

The key to success was to ensure there was nothing in my bags I didn't need. I had to be ruthless with my packing list as I considered what to bring and leave behind. Yet with careful planning, I managed. By the end of the trip, I think I had used every single item I'd brought. There were a few things I didn't bring but knew I could buy cheaply along the way as needed, but for the most part, I learned how to pack lightly and focus on what was most important.

That is what Jesus calls us to do as we follow him: pack lightly and focus on what is most important.

PRIORITIES

Almost every morning when I begin my quiet time with God, I pray the Lord's Prayer from Matthew 6. Often it takes several attempts before I get through the whole thing because I stop and start over again every time my mind wanders. I use this to center myself on God and focus on *his* priorities before I start reading his Word and talking to him about my needs. Essential to this process are the first few phrases.

Our Father in heaven ...

Immediately, I'm reminded that I am praying to God, my heavenly *Father!* Not just a god who insists on my obedience, but someone who *loves* me, disciplines me, and cares for my needs. He adopted me into his family by his grace and through the faith he gave me.

hallowed be your name ...

Equally important, I remember that God my Father is *holy.* He loves me more than I can imagine, but he is also wholly pure and righteous, perfect in goodness, above and beyond me, dwelling *"in unapproachable light"* (1 Timothy 6:16). This is the God to whom I pray, and it immediately humbles me and puts me back in my place.

Your kingdom come, your will be done, on earth as it is in heaven ...

This loving and holy God has infused this world with *purpose!* He's working history to cause his kingdom—his rule—to transpire throughout the whole world, just like it already is in heaven. I am reminded that God's purpose for this world is *my* purpose for living, so I choose to submit to him and do whatever most benefits his kingdom. I want everything I do today to be for his glory and purposes.

If I am focused on the king and his kingdom, everything unnecessary falls away.

NEEDS

Once I have centered myself on God and his priorities, my needs come properly into focus. These include my physical, spiritual, and relational needs.

Give us this day our daily bread ...

I acknowledge that I depend on God for all my *physical* needs. Note to self: bread is essential; Ferraris are not! As I pray, I am reminded to ask God to help me distinguish between what I need for each day and what I simply desire.

*and forgive us our debts ... and lead us not into temptation,
but deliver us from evil.*

My primary *spiritual* need is to be in a right relationship with God, to be forgiven, and to avoid any path that would lead me away from him. So every day I make sure that I confess my sins and get right with my Father.

as we also have forgiven our debtors ...

Finally, I'm reminded of my *relational* needs—to forgive others who may have intentionally or unintentionally hurt me with their words or actions. Jesus continues to say that God will forgive us if we forgive others, but if we refuse to forgive others, neither will we be forgiven. How sobering is that?

It's to our great benefit to acknowledge God's character and priorities and depend on him for all our needs. It comes down to submitting to him as Lord of every aspect of our lives.

STEWARDSHIP

So what do we do about all the *stuff?* Realistically, we need money and belongings in this world. It's not practical to give it all away and live like paupers. However, we must consider three vital biblical principles: stewardship, contentment, and generosity.

Unlike his only son, my dad was amazingly handy. He had all the equipment and knowledge to do woodworking, metalworking, welding, plumbing, electrical work, and car mechanics. As a paint chemist by trade, he even had a laboratory in the basement filled with chemicals, beakers, and devices. I have no idea what most of those were, but he did interesting things with them!

My dad also re-used whatever he could to save money, and there were bins of used nails, screws, gadgets, and all sorts of things. People would ask him if he happened to have an unusual item they needed to fix something, and he would say, "You know, I just might have one of those." Sure enough, ten minutes later, he'd often appear with the said item in hand!

He also had tons of tools, which he looked after very carefully. Each had its precise spot. He was generous and always willing to help, but I learned from a young age not to mess with his tools! If you borrowed them, you put them back where they belonged. I may have learned that the hard way once or twice when I was less careful with his tools than he was.

> **BONUS TIP:** Neither your tools *nor your father's tools* should be left out in the rain. Ever.

He was glad to lend me absolutely anything I needed and would gladly show me how to use each tool to fix my car or motorcycle, but I had to remember one thing—it was still *his*.

If I'm following Jesus, nothing I possess is truly mine. Not my money, family, house, car, talents, time, or the world around me. Yet I have certain responsibilities for all these things. The biblical word for this is *stewardship*. We are stewards of what God has lent us to use for his purposes and glory.

Traditionally, a steward was employed in a large estate to manage the property. They owned nothing in the estate but were responsible for how everything was looked after and administered. They supervised the servants, collected rent, and kept accounts correct. When their master arrived—at any time, night or day—the steward had to ensure everything was in order. Otherwise, they could be punished or removed from their position.

Joseph is an excellent example of a steward in the Bible. He was bought as a slave, rose to prominence in the house of Potiphar, and was made chief steward: "*So Joseph found favor in his sight and attended him, and he made him overseer of his house and put him in charge of all that he had*" (Genesis 39:4). However, Joseph *owned* nothing, and when it appeared that he had tried to seduce Potiphar's wife, he was thrown in prison immediately. His standing in the house was only at his master's pleasure, and when it seemed he had taken one of Potiphar's possessions—his wife—Joseph no longer had any standing. This was because none of it was his.

In Matthew 25, Jesus tells the parable of the talents. A master went away, and he gave three servants amounts of money to look after. Two of them invested it wisely and doubled the master's wealth, but the other servant buried the money and had nothing to show for what he had been entrusted with. The first two faithful servants were rewarded richly, but the third was cast out of the house and the master's presence. He was a poor steward of his master's resources.

The Apostle Peter wrote: "*Each of you should use whatever gift you have received to serve others, as faithful stewards of God's grace in its various forms*" (1 Peter 4:10, NIV). Whatever we have, whether treasures, talents, or time, it all belongs to God, and he will call each of us to account for it. Remember whose it is.

CONTENTMENT

My first job after college was with the One Way Adventure Foundation in the tiny town of Hedley, British Columbia. We looked after challenging teenagers who had broken the law or required foster care. In September 1990, I took my old, brown, 1973 four-door Mercury Comet, rented a U-Haul trailer, put almost everything I owned in it, and drove from Victoria to Hedley through the Cascade Mountains.

Unfortunately, there were some big hills, including a very steep incline from Hope to Sunshine Valley. The old Comet didn't like the extra weight it was pulling, and the radiator boiled over. Fortunately, I had some water with me, and eventually I got going again. Then it boiled over again on the next long stretch of hills, just before Sunday Summit. I had no water left this time and no idea what to do. Thank God there was a gravel pull-out and an RV sitting right there! The people inside gladly helped me out. My old Comet simply wasn't made to pull a load up steep hills. The trailer and all my possessions held it back from its purpose.

If I had wanted to be rich, I certainly wouldn't have gone to work in Hedley, especially given that I had just finished college and had student loans to pay off. It was a "missions" position, so I received $1,200 monthly. That would be equivalent to making about $12.50 an hour today. Not a lot, but it was sufficient. From that I still had to pay for room and board, yet I managed to save enough to pay off my student loans in that first year. Within two years, I saved $5,500 to buy a four-year-old Toyota Tercel that I kept for the next twelve years.

How did I do that? Simply put, I lived simply! I was content with little. As I had learned growing up, I seldom ate out and rarely bought anything I didn't specifically need. I still managed to give at least 10 percent of my income to help support the church I attended, and I also donated to additional important causes.

A hard lesson for most people is that *more* does not equal *happier*. I'm not saying that poverty is enjoyable. There's a level of wealth beneath which life can be truly miserable, and an increase in wealth will certainly improve those situations. However, beyond that level of basic *need*, getting more of what we want doesn't necessarily make us happier.

> BONUS TIP: You need far less than you think. Try living with less for a while. You may enjoy it and increase your appreciation for what you have.

The Apostle Paul was persecuted, beaten, shipwrecked, and imprisoned during much of his time following Jesus. While in prison, he wrote these words:

> *I rejoice greatly in the Lord that at last you renewed your concern for me … I am not saying this because I am in need, for I have learned to be content whatever the circumstances. I know what it is to be in need, and I know what it is to have plenty. I have learned the secret of*

*being content in any and every situation, whether well fed
or hungry, whether living in plenty or in want. I can do
all this through him who gives me strength.* (Philippians
4:10–13, NIV)

Paul said it didn't matter how much he had or even what circumstance
he faced; he had learned to be *content*. Why? How? Through the presence
of Jesus Christ in his life, who gave him the strength to be satisfied with
his situation. Similarly, the writer of Hebrews says, *"Keep your life free
from love of money, and be content with what you have, for he has said, 'I
will never leave you nor forsake you"* (Hebrews 13:5). Those are incredible
words! We can be content with little to nothing because we always have
Jesus with us. God's presence in our lives is better than stuff!

When the Israelites finally reached the Promised Land, each tribe
was allotted land according to their size and needs. However, the Levites,
who served in the Temple, received no land. What a rip-off! Here they
were, serving God, and after all the years and trouble of getting to their
new home and conquering their enemies, there was no land for them.
None. I'd be choked.

Or would I? The Bible tells us they received something even better:
God himself. What?

*The Levitical priests, all the tribe of Levi, shall have no
portion or inheritance with Israel ... They shall have
no inheritance among their brothers; the Lord is their
inheritance, as he promised them.* (Deuteronomy
18:1a–2, emphasis added)

In a world where land ownership was the greatest form of wealth,
the Levites were left out—and were blessed even more. Above all the
other tribes, they had the privilege of spending their lives in God's
presence, serving him.

The secret of contentment is to be near God and allow his presence
to dwell in us. No one can ever take that from you, whatever situation
you're in. That's what it means to travel light—you need nothing except

God looking out for you, Jesus at your side, and the Holy Spirit in your heart.

GENEROSITY

I have always tried to be generous with what I have because I know it all belongs to God. He also has taught me generosity through the actions of others when I've been in need. Compared to many of my peers, I had very little throughout my childhood, Bible school years, and early career, starting in Hedley. Yet God always provided.

I used to host guest groups for ski retreats in Hedley, and I'd drive them up to Apex Alpine ski hill in a big four-wheel-drive bus. I bought some used skis, boots, and poles to ski with the groups for some of the time. One day, after cleaning up after the lunch I'd packed for everyone, I went to get my skis, and they were missing! After a long search, I could only conclude that they had been stolen. But why *mine* when there were so many much nicer pairs around?

It was just the beginning of the ski season, and that very next week, I had a youth group coming to ski, so not having skiis was very disheartening. Not only could I not afford another pair of skis, but I didn't have the time to drive somewhere to find some. Yet God knew what I needed, and that very next weekend, the group leader arrived at our camp with a pair of skis for me. Someone—and I never found out who—learned about my loss, found me a used pair similar to my old ones, and donated them to me. Wow! I was so surprised and thankful! This is the way things have often gone in my life. When I most needed something, God provided through others.

When I was graduating from high school, I didn't own a suit, and my parents couldn't afford to buy me one, so my youth pastor gave me his old three-piece suit—to keep! It fit perfectly. Too bad it was grey, but I still looked pretty sharp, according to the photos.

That summer after graduating, I badly wanted to go on a three-week missions trip with our youth group. It would cost $550, and I simply couldn't afford it. Graduation fees were bad enough. I earned and saved what I could, but I still was $200 short. I was again amazed when a neighbor, not knowing how much I was lacking, donated $200 towards my trip—*exactly* what I still needed!

When I worked for Youth For Christ, I had to raise all my support, which was tough. Yet some people believed in what I was doing and donated generously. One of my biggest monthly donors was an older cousin I hardly knew. I wasn't sure I should even send him a fundraising letter, but I'm so glad I did. He donated $200 every month for years, and I have no idea how he afforded it because he certainly wasn't wealthy. He was such an example to me, even though I don't think he was following Christ at the time.

It probably sounds like I've been a charity case all my life, but that's not the case. I've always tried to earn whatever I needed, and God has come through in remarkable ways whenever I was short. The year Leanne and I had to move from our rental basement suite and hoped to buy a house, two incredible things happened. My grandmother left us a small inheritance, and my uncle gave us $25,000 out of the blue—he'd won a lottery! Not that I was happy to lose my grandmother, nor do I advocate gambling, but it was perfect timing. We also had a relative provide us with an interest-free loan for the rest.

As a result of the generosity I have received, I love to give to others in need. I was taught early on to donate 10 percent of whatever I received to God's ministries, and Leanne grew up with the same practice. However, after a few years of marriage, Leanne and I realized we were looking at things wrongly. If it's *all* God's, the question should never be how much we *give* but how much we *keep* for ourselves.

We realized that keeping 90 percent of what we received from various sources was far more than we needed to live on, so we increased our giving percentage significantly and continued to do so the more we received. We also realized that we had a lot of possessions, so over the last few years, we've been trying to give away things to people who might need them more than we do. This might sound generous, but we still have a way to go! Besides, the less we own, the less we need to worry about, find places for, be responsible for, and repair. Less stuff—simplicity—often means *more* happiness.

Better is the little that the righteous has than the abundance of many wicked. For the arms of the wicked shall be broken, but the Lord upholds the righteous. (Psalm 37:16–17)

[G]ive, and it will be given to you. Good measure, pressed down, shaken together, running over, will be put into your lap. For with the measure you use it will be measured back to you. (Luke 6:38)

We don't give to God to receive back from him, yet when we're generous, we find that somehow it does come back, often in spiritual blessings. We can never out-give our generous Father.

> BONUS TIP: Generosity often leads to unexpected joy. I have been surprised when God has taken my gift and done something amazing with it, like meeting a need I didn't even know about.

LETTING GO

I'm not saying God wants us to be poor, just the right kind of rich. He never tells us *not* to seek treasures; he tells us to seek the *right* treasures: *lasting* ones. He would not be a loving God if he advised us to seek things that don't satisfy or last.

Sell your possessions, and give to the needy. Provide yourselves with moneybags that do not grow old, with a treasure in the heavens that does not fail, where no thief approaches and no moth destroys. For where your treasure is, there will your heart be also. (Luke 12:33–34)

In some ways, letting go of your stuff and your desire to be rich on this earth is purely selfish because it will mean contentment and joy in this life *and* in the life to come!

My family was hiking above Lake Louise in Alberta a few years ago. As usual, I carried a backpack with everyone's water bottles and extra items. It was a steep hike almost the whole way, and by the time we reached Lake Agnes (and a way-cool tea house), we were all exhausted. The plan was only to hike to the lake, but when I took off my backpack, I suddenly had this urge to hike up another twenty minutes to a viewpoint I saw on the map.

No one else was game to go, so I left the backpack with them and somehow *jogged* up the hill to the viewpoint! I took a few photos and then ran back down, and the whole extra trip took less than half an hour. My family was surprised that I had so much energy after the steep hike, but they were no more amazed than I was. It came down to two things: I got rid of my excess baggage, and I badly wanted to see the view from the top. I was so glad I did!

If we can focus on what is worthwhile and eliminate excess baggage, we'll have more than we ever dreamed of. The trick to traveling light is keeping our priorities right by fixing our eyes on Jesus and his purposes. We need to practice letting go—of having open hands to God with all our possessions.

I think this is one place the Western church has gotten it wrong. It has become spiritually acceptable and even noble for Christians to accumulate wealth *in this world* for their own gratification. Where did we get that idea? It certainly isn't found in New Testament Christianity.

Furthermore—we will talk more on this later—we need to let go of anything else that weighs us down, especially sin, guilt, broken relationships, and a lack of forgiveness. Anything that gets in the way of doing what God has called us to do—love him and love others— must be removed. Yet many Christians have never been taught this. And many of those who know it to be accurate are unwilling to let go.

What will it take for you to let go and follow Christ?

CHOOSE YOUR OWN ADVENTURE

The Wise Path: I choose to make God's priorities my priorities, leaving behind anything that distracts me from his purposes.

The Foolish Path: I choose to seek and hold on to things that can never satisfy my deepest longings.

— Chapter Four —
WHEN THE GOING GETS TOUGH

Many are the afflictions of the righteous,
but the Lord delivers him out of them all.
~Psalm 34:19

A long the paths of life, there will be magnificent, sunny days when everything is going well, and there will be horrible, stormy days when you manage to trip over every root and fall into every mudhole. Sometimes you wish you had stayed home.

If there's something truly universal to everyone who has ever walked on this planet, it's the experience of hardships and suffering. From when we're old enough to jam a finger in our crib until our final—sometimes gasping—breath, we all experience pain, loss, and sorrow.

The good news for the believer is that even our best days in this world will be worse than any day to come after we die. Yet for those who refuse to bow a knee to Jesus, today's worst days are but a shadow of the horrors to come. May we each find Jesus Christ, the narrow gate, before it's too late.

TOUGH TIMES

In my first year of Bible college, I started to have significant abdominal pain. After many tests, I was diagnosed with ulcerative colitis, which was later upgraded to Crohn's disease. Being far from home and learning to cope with an awful sickness was tough.

I'm on some good medications now, but it's often a struggle, and some days are particularly rough. I've learned over time to cope, and by

God's grace alone, I have even managed to work in stressful ministry positions over these past thirty-plus years.

Not long after Leanne and I married, I was encouraged to apply as an associate pastor at a small community church, mainly to work with youth. We stepped out in faith, applied, went through all the hoops, and somehow passed the church vote with about 96 percent in favor. That seemed to be a high percentage in favor, but I certainly wondered who that 4 percent were that didn't want me there! I didn't think I'd be a good pastor, but after much prayer and counsel, we believed God was leading us on this path.

As I was about to start, I had a somewhat disconcerting discussion with someone who had recently been a volunteer youth leader at the church. He warned me that this would be an incredibly difficult ministry and to be very careful, especially around certain youths' parents he did not name. However, having had success in almost everything I had attempted in life until then, I believed I would succeed where others had failed. God had called me, and I would thrive! Though disguised as faith in God, I now recognize this was immature pride.

BONUS TIP: Never ignore the warnings and advice of people who have walked the trail ahead of you.

Things started well, and I began to get to know the junior and senior youth group members. I was especially eager to disciple and teach them from God's Word, and many responded very favorably to my leadership and teaching. As typical, some were more interested in having fun than in learning and growing.

Just a month after I started, my son, Ben, was born, bringing me a new level of exhaustion. I also began to get resistance from certain parents on the board who disagreed with how I was doing things. I later found out that they were the ones who had voted against my coming. Knowing what I do now about boards, I have no idea how I was called in the first place if the board was not in complete agreement.

Furthermore, not understanding small churches or church politics, I made a few accidental missteps along the way, and soon I was under heavy fire from these parents. Due to the stress, my lack of sleep, and my now very active Crohn's disease, my health deteriorated. After only seven months of pouring my life and love into those kids, I felt I had no option but to resign. It was one of the toughest decisions I've ever made. How could I leave what God had called me to, especially when I was making such great progress with so many teens?

FROM BAD TO WORSE

The week I handed in my resignation letter, I went to see a surgeon about a pain I'd been having in my abdomen for some time, which I assumed was from my Crohn's disease. He decided it was a hernia and had a sudden opening that week if I wanted to get it repaired immediately. Or I could wait for about three weeks if I'd rather. I decided to get it done, so I missed my last Sunday in that church.

When they opened me up to repair the hernia, they found that my appendix was severely swollen, wrapped up in my bowel, and ready to burst. It's a good thing I hadn't waited a few more weeks! That surgery led to further complications with my Crohn's, and I soon formed a severe infection—a sinus tract—in my bowel.

Six tough months after my appendectomy, I required a major operation to remove a large part of my colon. I felt so rotten I was glad to finally have the surgery and get it over with. As I lay on the bed about to be anesthetized, I asked the doctor how long they were putting me out for. I don't remember how long it was, but my last thought before going out was, *That's cutting it close*—excuse the pun—because I thought my surgery was supposed to take at least that long.

My next conscious thought was—and I quote—*Aaaaaaaahhhhhh!* My anesthesia had worn off right when they moved me from the operating table to a gurney, and I remember waking up screaming in pain. Fortunately, they put me on morphine. I was placed in a mini-ICU for the next few days while they monitored my initial recovery. When my poor wife came to see me, I was looking rough and talking nonsense due to the drugs. Strangely, part of my brain was listening to the nonsense I was uttering, and I later remembered some of what I'd said—to my complete embarrassment!

Over the next week, I suffered immense pain, discomfort, and weakness. It was truly awful. Hospital food is ordinarily bad enough, but I could only eat clear fluids and items labeled "bland." I was too miserable to enjoy visitors. The hospital was noisy, night and day, and I would finally fall asleep just in time to be woken up by nurses going off-duty and taking my vitals or blood samples, or giving me medications.

> BONUS TIP: Although a hospital staff works very hard to look after every patient, there are limits to what they can do in their busyness. Never assume your loved ones are getting the care they need; ask questions if you're unsure.

When I was released, I still wasn't doing well. It was so discouraging three days later to return to the hospital for another few days of recovery.

When I was finally fit to be home again, Leanne had to return to work, leaving me with a one-year-old to look after. Physically it was tough, but emotionally and spiritually, I felt abandoned by God, like I'd messed up, and he was done with me. We also had left our church and friendship groups and were uncomfortable returning.

The worst was the irrational belief that I was a complete failure and that no one would ever hire me for a ministry position again. I felt like God was done with me and had left me on a shelf. The physical healing took about a year, but my sadness and bitterness were around much longer.

UNDERSTANDING SUFFERING

What do you do when your life blows up? Where do you go when everything you believed and bet your life on seems to be proven useless? How do you keep going when the path turns to brambles?

A year after my operation, Leanne had our second child, Lorelle, and Leanne was now eligible for a year of maternity leave. We decided it was a good time for me to return to school. I began my Master of Theological Studies degree at Northwest Baptist Seminary, where I made good friends and enjoyed lively discussions on many practical biblical topics. It was an excellent opportunity to learn and grow.

> BONUS TIP: I was worried that seminary would be very difficult, but I found it easier academically than Bible college. Don't be afraid to pursue graduate studies after completing an undergraduate degree.

During this time, Lorelle began to get very sick, and eventually she was also diagnosed with Crohn's disease, which is very rare for someone only a couple of years old. My heart was broken, thinking about the suffering she would likely have in store, and I began to explore the subject of suffering more seriously at school.

I took an elective called Theology of Suffering. This drove me to spend many hours reading Christian books on suffering, studying the Word, and writing papers on this critical subject. When it came time to write my master's thesis, I also chose the topic of suffering. Specifically, I focused on the Apostle Paul's understanding of the suffering of the righteous. This meant further months of research and writing on the subject. Eventually, I completed a 145-page project with ninety-eight books listed in the bibliography, all of which I had studied to help me understand this topic. This can be found under "Resources" on my website: cwdouglas.com.

I suppose I should have been an expert in the field by then, and I did learn a lot. But in many ways, I feel like I only scooped up a spoonful of water in the ocean of God's plan in allowing suffering. The rest of this chapter is about some of the lessons I learned: first, why suffering exists, and second, how we should deal with it.

To begin to understand suffering, we need to consider at least three essential principles.

1. Sin Is the Root of Suffering

All suffering has the evil of sin at its root. God made a perfect world and allowed people to choose whether or not to obey him. When they chose to rebel, this brought sin and suffering into the world (see Genesis 3). We suffer because creation itself is fallen due to sin.

This doesn't mean there's always a *direct* correlation between a particular sin and specific suffering, but rather all who live in this fallen world will necessarily experience the effects of a creation marred by sin. This is seen in Jesus's responses in Luke 13:1–5.

> *There were some present at that very time who told him about the Galileans whose blood Pilate had mingled with their sacrifices. And he answered them, "Do you think that these Galileans were worse sinners than all the other Galileans, because they suffered in this way? No, I tell you; but unless you repent, you will all likewise perish. Or those eighteen on whom the tower in Siloam fell and killed them: do you think that they were worse offenders than all the others who lived in Jerusalem? No, I tell you; but unless you repent, you will all likewise perish."*

People often suffer simply because we live in a fallen world. However, some suffering is the direct result of particular sins. Those who ignore God's call for monogamous relationships are more likely to catch sexually transmitted diseases. Robbers are sometimes shot. Speeders are sometimes injured or killed in car accidents. However, there's not always a direct link between sin and suffering. A blood transfusion can cause a disease, a bystander may be shot, and someone obeying the traffic laws may be injured or killed in a car accident.

All have sinned, and therefore everyone *deserves* to suffer punishment—and death—in general. It doesn't follow that suffering is always a direct result of a particular sin; however, the righteous, more than any, must expect to suffer because they live in a world opposed to God. They also follow a Lord who, though perfect, also suffered at the hands of sinful men. Jesus warned his followers that they would likewise suffer.

2. Suffering Is Universal

Part of my thesis research involved identifying the numerous terms used for suffering in Paul's writings in the New Testament. What I thought would be a straightforward exercise required several weeks of study.

In Paul's thirteen epistles, I found seventy-nine different Greek root words referring to suffering! With their derivatives (various forms of the same word), Paul uses many of these up to one hundred times each. Clearly, suffering is one of the primary themes in the thirteen books of the Bible he wrote, and the rest of the New Testament treats it similarly.

This is likely because suffering is one of *the* most universal experiences, possibly the most universal. Living in this broken world, none of us can escape various kinds of affliction, which is why the biblical authors mentioned it regularly and often.

> **BONUS TIP:** It's often helpful to remember that we're not alone in our miseries. Others have gone through it before, and most have been made stronger through it all.

3. Suffering Is Often *Made* Beneficial

It's easy to miss that although God doesn't *cause* suffering, he often takes suffering and uses it to accomplish extraordinary things.

> *As he passed by, he saw a man blind from birth. And his disciples asked him, "Rabbi, who sinned, this man or his parents, that he was born blind?" Jesus answered, "It was not that this man sinned, or his parents, but that the works of God might be displayed in him."* (John 9:1–3)

Note that this man's suffering was not a result of his own sins or those of his parents. God allowed this man to suffer blindness—from birth!— for purposes he couldn't understand until much later. Eventually, we see that his blindness led to a relationship with Jesus and eternal life. I love this man's simple testimony after being badgered by the religious leaders about who had performed this miracle: *"One thing I do know, that though I was blind, now I see"* (John 9:25b).

In my many months of studying, I discovered that God uses suffering for many purposes. These include sanctifying believers (making them more holy), teaching them, disciplining them, helping them to learn to rely on him, and causing them to identify more closely with Jesus. God also uses suffering to benefit his Church: unifying it, encouraging it, and building it up, especially as Christians see other believers persevere and flourish amid trials.

God can take even a great evil like suffering and bring good from it.

COMFORTED TO COMFORTER

When I returned to the hospital the second time, something interesting happened. I wasn't well enough to be at home, but I became much stronger than I had been the previous week. I began to look at those suffering around me, and instead of feeling sorry for myself, I started to feel compassion for them.

> **BONUS TIP:** One great way to alleviate your own discomfort, when you can, is to take the focus off yourself and see the difficulties of others around you.

God used me to talk to others and share his love and gospel with people in my room and even visitors I met on my walks down the hallway. I even had the opportunity to pray with some people worried about their family member in the hospital. What happened? I went from being the victim to ministering to others. I think it has to do with what we read in 2 Corinthians 1:3–4:

> Blessed be the God and Father of our Lord Jesus Christ, the Father of mercies and God of all comfort, who comforts us in all our affliction, so that we may be able to comfort those who are in any affliction, with the comfort with which we ourselves are comforted by God.

As God comforted me in my afflictions that first week, I learned how to comfort others with *his* comfort!

This is one of those things that amazes me about knowing Jesus. What we may assume is meaningless, such as suffering, God takes and somehow redeems. He can redeem even the worst circumstances to bring himself glory and honor and to draw others closer to him. He exchanges *"beauty for ashes"* (Isaiah 61:3, NLT).

RESPONDING TO SUFFERING

Given that we will experience suffering in this world, it's critical to know how to respond to it. Most people tend to either lash out or give up. Neither of these responses helps the situation, but what can we do?

If we start with an understanding that suffering is permitted by God for his divine purposes, it can change our perspective. Here are some essential concepts to help us deal wisely with suffering.

1. Prepare for the Storm

When you're out on the trail, it's helpful to know when inclement weather is on the way. At times when I've been camping in the backcountry, I've known that it was going to rain hard, so I've worn appropriate clothing, prepared tarps, and gathered dry wood ahead of time. I can't stop the rain from coming, but I can mitigate its impact on me.

We usually don't know when pain and misery will come, but we know it *is* coming and may be right around the corner. Jesus told his followers, *"In the world you will have tribulation. But take heart; I have overcome the world"* (John 16:33b). Similarly, Peter wrote, *"Beloved, do not be surprised at the fiery trial when it comes upon you to test you, as though something strange were happening to you"* (1 Peter 4:12).

Since we know suffering is coming, the wise response is to prepare ourselves and each other. Yet as soon as things get tough, Christians often act as if God has abandoned them. They act like their world has been completely rocked when trials come their way.

Are we living in a dangerously sanitized society, where the slightest headache or itch can be solved with a pill or a cream, where we keep our children from seeing the homeless, the sick, and the dying? We need to talk about suffering in our homes, take our kids to hospitals and funerals, study what the Bible says about suffering, teach about it from the pulpit, read about Christian martyrs, and accept this reality. Otherwise, it will catch us off-guard, and we will be ill-prepared to handle it.

2. Understand the Body as Our Model for Care

As discussed earlier, we need one another. On our own, the trail is much more dangerous and less enjoyable.

God has given us one another to help us through this life. As the Apostle Paul explains in 1 Corinthians 12, we are one body, and Christ is the head of the body. Each part is necessary for the function of the whole body. No one should act as if they don't need the others, nor should they act as if they're not needed.

> *But God has so composed the body, giving greater honor to the part that lacked it, that there may be no division in the body, but* that the members may have the same care for one another. If one member suffers, all suffer together; *if one member is honored, all rejoice together.* (1 Corinthians 12:24b–26, emphasis added)

We all know that if one part of our body hurts, it affects the rest of our body. You stub a toe or get something in your eye, and it affects your whole person. Furthermore, the rest of the body compensates for the hurt. When I tore my knee ligament in soccer, my healthy leg worked hard for many weeks to compensate and lessen the pain of my injured leg.

> BONUS TIP: If you have a massive brace on your leg, and people in your church complain because you were "wearing shorts on the stage while reading scripture," there's something wrong with those people. Don't be like that!

Similarly, when one part of the body hurts or is weak, the other parts hurt with that part and do what they can to alleviate the pain. We're also instructed to *"bear one another's burdens"* (Galatians 6:2).

No one should be left to suffer on their own. As the body of Christ, we're to care for one another and share God's love and comfort with those who don't know him. This is part of our witness to the world.

Imagine the difference it would make if the Church was known for caring for one another rather than complaining about all the sins in society! Imagine if the church was the first place people thought to go when troubled because "those people really care." Yet that was Jesus' plan for the Church, his body.

3. Acquire a Language of Lament

When we first face loss or tragedy in our lives, it's very difficult to express our feelings. We're overwhelmed, and it takes time to wrap our minds around what has happened and how we feel about it.

A few years ago, I lost a good friend and co-worker named Dan to cancer. Week after week, I visited him in the hospital and watched him deteriorate. His wife, Evelyn, was a good friend, and we sat with her in church each week and tried to support her as best we could. It was tough to sing in church, especially since most songs were celebratory. One song we sang in particular, "Sovereign over Us" by Michael W. Smith, was impactful during that time. It talks about how God meets us in our suffering and teaches us how to trust him, even when we don't understand why things are happening. God has not forgotten us but remains forever faithful in his sovereignty.

Even thinking about that today, I feel the impact of those words, and I have tears in my eyes as I think of Dan and how God met all of us in our sorrow and was sovereign throughout the situation. I remember how Dan, unable to speak because of the cancer in his throat, would write on paper or type on his phone to tell us that he was okay and was continuing to trust in the Lord, no matter what happened. I remember how his eyes would light up and tear up when I read scripture to him. He knew he would probably die, but he kept expressing his faith in Jesus.

He passed into the Lord's presence at thirty-eight years old, leaving behind a wife and two young children. He was our food services manager and campfire leader at Timberline Ranch for about fifteen years, dearly loved by hundreds of campers, staff members, and volunteers. At his graveside, I sobbed, overwhelmed. The next day, I managed to deliver a eulogy at his funeral. Expressing my feelings was hard, but even writing those words helped some.

Over the next many months, I tried to come to grips with what had happened, and I wrote a song about Dan called "Unsung Hero." It took months of writing and re-writing to get it just right. It was my way of honoring him and what God had done through him. Performing the song at camp that summer was incredibly challenging at first, but I think it helped me and others deal with our deep sense of loss.

For people to recover from the shock of tragedy or affliction, they need to be able to express their feelings. We see this clearly in the Psalms and other parts of scripture, where the rawness of life, anger, disappointment, and frustration are expressed. Paul himself conveyed his feelings to God and to the churches to whom he wrote. For example, he expressed *"great sorrow and unceasing anguish"* in his heart at the plight of his unsaved fellow Jews (Romans 9:2).

Yet many churches have discarded any liturgy containing the language of lament and sorrow. Our songs are most often upbeat and celebratory, and we seldom hear sermons on the lament passages in scripture, despite their frequency. Take Psalm 22, for example, which begins,

> *My God, my God, why have you forsaken me?*
> *Why are you so far from saving me,*
> *so far from my cries of anguish?*
> *My God, I cry out by day, but you do not answer,*
> *by night, but I find no rest.* (Psalm 22:1–2, NIV)

Where is there room to express sorrow, frustration, and fear that God has abandoned us in our suffering? We must not ignore pain or avoid the language of grief. We must regain some of these methods that our spiritual ancestors found helpful. People need to know that it's acceptable and a healthy part of recovery to voice their complaints, fears, and longings to God.

4. Develop a "Mature Acceptance" of Suffering

There's a time to fight suffering and a time to accept it. We must avoid the two extremes of either *prematurely* accepting the inevitability of suffering or *never* accepting it. The Apostle Paul displayed a healthy balance of this in his personal suffering:

> *So to keep me from becoming conceited because of the surpassing greatness of the revelations, a thorn was given me in the flesh, a messenger of Satan to harass me, to keep me from becoming conceited. Three times I pleaded with the Lord about this, that it should leave me.* (2 Corinthians 12:7–8)

Paul knew that suffering was inevitable as part of the fallen state of this world and as a direct result of sin. He was willing to endure suffering for the sake of his Lord. Yet when facing his awful "*thorn in the flesh*," Paul prayed fervently, pleadingly, for God to take it away. He says he prayed "*three times*," which probably should be understood as three *seasons* of intense prayer.

When presented with suffering—whether ours or someone else's—we should do all we reasonably can to reduce or eliminate it. Seek medical help, use medicine, and go for treatments as applicable. However, there often comes a time when we need to accept that this is God's permissive will. Paul continues:

> *But he said to me, "My grace is sufficient for you, for my power is made perfect in weakness." Therefore I will boast all the more gladly of my weaknesses, so that the power of Christ may rest upon me. For the sake of Christ, then, I am content with weaknesses, insults, hardships, persecutions, and calamities. For when I am weak, then I am strong.* (2 Corinthians 12:9–10)

Paul didn't want to suffer. He was not a masochist! But over time, after praying hard and hearing from God, he accepted it as *within* God's will for him. He chose to be content with it as part of God's plan. He realized that God was shown to be powerful through his weaknesses.

A mature acceptance of suffering over time doesn't mean giving up but trusting in God's purposes. Like Paul, I have experienced God's presence and strength more through suffering than in any other way. I currently have four diagnosed chronic illnesses plus an undiagnosed sleeping disorder. Medications help somewhat, and I seek to improve my situation as I can, but I also experience God's pure grace every day, especially on my worst ones.

We should never flippantly accept or ignore suffering. However, when all has been done that reasonably can be done, we need to choose to trust God, receive his peace, *"which surpasses all understanding"* (Philippians 4:7), and remember that he is with us.

5. Suffer Alongside Others

As followers of Jesus, we have a calling to love one another and be compassionate, just as he is. This means that we are willing to "suffer with" or "suffer alongside" others, which is what "compassion" literally means. Jesus set the example and continues to suffer alongside us: *"When [Jesus] went ashore he saw a great crowd, and he had compassion on them, because they were like sheep without a shepherd"* (Mark 6:34a); *"As a father shows compassion to his children, so the Lord shows compassion to those who fear him"* (Psalm 103:13).

To be compassionate means joining another in their suffering and taking their burdens as our own. One of the best things we can do for others is simply to be *present* for them. It's often counterproductive to try to find answers for them. We may be called to look for cures and solutions for a time, but that should never be a substitute for simply being present and walking with them through their pain and sorrow. Hurting people need our presence more than our solutions.

When my friend Dan was dying in the hospital, we did all we could for him in prayer and medically, yet at some point, we knew he wouldn't make it without a miracle. So we continued to pray and simply spent time at his side, loving and caring for him. Evelyn and I even managed to play a board game with him on his last birthday, shortly before he died, moving the pieces for him. It was so hard to be with him like that, but it was what he needed and what I would have wanted in his situation.

Compassion is costly, but it's what we're called to give to those who suffer—just like God has given us.

6. Confront Evil Where Possible

I've had many encounters with bears over the years. I see them regularly at our camp and sometimes when I'm hiking. I'm quite used to them and often chase them off to keep them from frightening our guests. We also do everything possible to avoid having full garbage cans or food left anywhere it might attract them.

Bears certainly are not evil—I am thrilled when I see them—but they can't be left to wander around the camp to terrorize campers or possibly harm them. So we drive them away. Similarly, suffering is never welcome in our lives, and we're wise to do what we can to remove it, avoid it, or drive it far away.

At times we need to *confront* evil. Much suffering directly results from evil oppressors and systems that harm people. Prominent examples include abusers, pimps, drug lords, slave owners, and oppressive regimes. We must be willing to put our lives on the line to set captives free—to confront those who intentionally harm others. Yet this must also be done with a genuine love for the oppressors, as difficult as that may be. Compassion demands that we understand that they are also slaves to sin and need God's freeing love.

I believe God calls certain people to positions and places where they can make a difference and change oppressive systems. I think of people like William Wilberforce, a Christian politician in England who worked most of his life to abolish the British slave trade. Against seemingly impossible odds and overcoming intense opposition, God used him to change the course of history and emancipate thousands, if not millions, of slaves.

BONUS TIP: Read some of the many great Christian biographies available. They will inspire you and help your faith grow. We have a collection of over fifty, and they've

been a great help in our family's faith development. (See
cwdouglas.com for some suggested biographies)

Not all of us are in that position or have that kind of opportunity,
but we can be aware of the evil around us and pray. As we pray, God may
use *us* as part of his answer to bring about change.

At the same time, we must avoid running ahead of God and losing
sight of the mission he has given us to make disciples. Despite living
under an oppressive and corrupt Roman system of government, neither
Paul nor Jesus confronted that system or tried to change it directly. This
was not the mission to which either was called.

Constant prayer is our best and most foundational weapon against
evil in this world, and that is undoubtedly the place to start. But we
also need to pay attention to God's Spirit so that when we have the
opportunity to step in and confront evil, we're ready to do so, despite
what it may cost us.

7. Focus on True Hope

Above all else, we must offer hope to those who suffer. We know that
despair increases suffering and worsens even physical ailments, yet hope is
shown to help people keep going. People need to be pointed to God for
help, strength, and perseverance.

One morning, four-and-a-half years after my perceived failure as a
pastor, I woke up knowing something was different inside me. It was
gone—the bitterness, fear, and discouragement I had struggled with.
Somehow, God replaced it with joy and genuine hope for the future.
It was as if he had simply stepped in and removed something from me
overnight, and I knew it was an answer to many prayers.

Though I still suffered physically from Crohn's and other ailments,
those feelings never returned, and I was finally able to move forward.
Just a year later, I was finally ready to go back into ministry, into the
position I've now held for over eighteen years.

Believers need to see that there is hope, not only for eternity but
also for today. They need to understand that God has a bigger plan than

we can see, and he can use suffering to accomplish much greater things than we can imagine.

Philippians, known as the most joyful book in the Bible, was written by Paul while he suffered in a Roman prison. Observe Paul's joy in these words:

> *Rejoice in the Lord always; again I will say, rejoice. Let your reasonableness be known to everyone. The Lord is at hand; do not be anxious about anything, but in everything by prayer and supplication with thanksgiving let your requests be made known to God. And the peace of God, which surpasses all understanding, will guard your hearts and your minds in Christ Jesus.* (Philippians 4:4–7)

There are no *easy* answers to suffering, but there *are* answers. God's Word makes it clear that he takes what the enemy means for evil and makes good come from it. He has not abandoned us, and he will bring us through these circumstances in his time. Better days are coming!

> *For I consider that* the sufferings of this present time *are not worth comparing with the glory that is to be revealed to us. For the creation waits with eager longing for the revealing of the sons of God. For the creation was subjected to futility, not willingly, but because of him who subjected it,* in hope that the creation itself will be set free *from its bondage to corruption and obtain the freedom of the glory of the children of God …*
>
> *And we know* that for those who love God all things work together for good, *for those who are called according to his purpose …*
>
> *No,* in all these things we are more than conquerors through him who loved us. *For I am sure that neither death nor life, nor angels nor rulers, nor things present nor things to come, nor powers, nor height nor depth, nor anything else in all creation, will be able to separate us*

from the love of God in Christ Jesus our Lord. (Romans 8:18–21, 28, 37–39, emphasis added)

CHOOSE YOUR OWN ADVENTURE

The Wise Path: I choose to trust God's goodness and sovereignty amid suffering, believing he can redeem it for his glorious purposes.

The Foolish Path: I choose to blame God for the pain and suffering I face, missing out on his comfort and plan.

Chapter Five

COMPANIONS ON THE TRAIL

One who is righteous is a guide to his neighbor,
but the way of the wicked leads them astray.
~Proverbs 12:26

Second only to our relationship with the God of the universe is the importance of having good people in our lives who can encourage us and help us stay on the narrow path. After all, the trail is sweetest when it can be shared with people you love and who love you.

Unfortunately, that is never a given.

Growing up, I had many so-called friends, guys I enjoyed being around and who seemingly enjoyed being around me. Mostly, we shared a love for sports, so we spent lots of our time playing street hockey or soccer, though we also played football, softball, tennis, and basketball or rode our bikes through the woods and over jumps. It was a great way to grow up.

In the summer, I was that guy phoning up everyone I knew—and somewhat liked—to get together in the park to play some sports. Sometimes we'd get a dozen kids or more and could play a softball game. Usually, someone would get mad or hurt in one of our games, but in the end, we went home exhausted and glad we'd played together.

I was good at organizing people but wasn't necessarily a great friend. I cared more about myself than I did others. If it was more fun to play with John than Richard, then "So long, Richard." If others were laughing at a kid in our class who we thought talked funny or wasn't very coordinated, I sometimes joined in. I even got into fistfights—with my "friends"!

It's easy to think, *Well, that's just the way kids are.* But I certainly knew better. A lot of my behavior was simply wrong. I have many regrets about how I treated some of my classmates and went along with the crowd. I was fortunate to have some decent friends.

All that changed when I reached junior high (grade eight). Suddenly, I was in a huge school, and I wasn't with any of my friends in my homeroom or classes. They all began to make new friends, and I didn't connect well with anyone in my classes. My old friends hung out with kids who swore and made crude jokes non-stop, so I didn't want to be with them. But I had to join them if I didn't want to eat my lunch alone. They tolerated me, and I tolerated them, but I was lonely.

Worst of all, I began having knee and back problems that plagued me throughout high school, and I couldn't play on the school sports teams. At the risk of sounding dramatic, I felt alone on the trail and in grave danger of getting lost.

If it hadn't been for our church youth group, I could have been in big trouble. There I found acceptance, friends, and role models. The group was mostly girls, and I didn't mind that so much by then.

NEW APPRECIATION

When I was in grade eleven, Dale started coming to our youth group. He was nothing like me. He was tall, blond, pale, and unathletic. He was friendly enough, but I was busy being "important" by helping run the youth group. Did I mention there were a *lot* of girls in the youth group?

Out of the blue one Sunday afternoon, Dale phoned me and asked if I'd like to come to his house and hang out. My first thought was, *Oh, great. Hanging out with someone with whom I have nothing in common, trapped at their house? No, thank you!* This was precisely the kind of social situation I wanted to avoid.

But then I thought, *What a brave guy to phone someone he hardly knows and invite him over.* I also had a conviction that the Holy Spirit was saying, "Go!" So I went. It was initially awkward, but Dale had some computer games, and we managed to get through the time. From then on, we became, well, acquaintances. I tried to include him a little more at the youth group, but I had other things going on, and he wasn't a priority.

One evening at youth group, a guy started to make fun of Dale and call him names. My blood began to boil. I had been picked on by older kids when I was younger, and I'd developed this *thing* about bullies. So I immediately started defending Dale and nearly got in a fistfight—at youth group! Why? I didn't fully know. I think I felt sorry for Dale, but the truth is, he was an extremely nice guy, and I had begun to appreciate him for who he was—intelligent, witty, and fun.

The strange thing was that Dale somehow became my best friend over the next year or so! He went to my high school in my final year, worked at camp with me for a couple of summers, and attended Bible college with me for four years. We were, in many ways, inseparable. He was generous, kind, and accepting—precisely what a friend should be. And I think he helped me learn what it meant to be a good friend.

> BONUS TIP: People who aren't very much like you sometimes make great friends when you enjoy some of the same things or have similar senses of humor.

FRIENDSHIPS

When I was younger, I always had to like someone to be their friend. That probably makes sense in one way but is entirely backward in another. One of the reasons I didn't always have good friends was that I had to learn what it meant to *be* a good friend.

When we're young, we tend to gravitate towards those who can meet *our* need for acceptance—people who make us feel understood and are kind to us. Over time, wise people learn that friendship is worth little unless it's also about what we give to others. Perhaps unsurprisingly, we generally get the most out of relationships where we give the most. We also tend to attract the kind of friends we are to others.

It seems obvious, but how many of us settle for friends who aren't good for us? How many of us have been so desperate for friendship that we hung out with people we didn't even like? You've probably heard of the "Golden Rule" Jesus gave in Matthew 7:12: "*So in everything, do to others what you would have them do to you ...*" (NIV). Most people think of this altruistically—that we should treat others well, no matter how they treat us. Yet practically, kindness to others may also attract kind people to be our friends.

Unfortunately, there is no guarantee that others will treat you well if you treat them well. Jesus loved and showed kindness to everyone, yet those same people had him killed for crimes he didn't commit. Sometimes we can be good friends to others and still be hurt by those who don't reciprocate. Some people are afraid of getting close, many are self-centered, and others may simply not know how to be good friends.

Regardless, treating people with love and kindness is the best approach if we want to attract good friends. Go out of your way to invite them into your life, and you will sometimes see that reciprocated.

I used to love that although Dale and I had little money, when we went out for coffee, one of us always paid for both. If we were unsure who had paid last, both would immediately offer to pay. In fact, we would *compete* to pay! It was a healthy way for us to say, "You are valuable, and I want to put you first."

PUTTING OTHERS FIRST

When I got married, I wanted to ensure I was doing my fair share of the housework because I knew my natural desire would be to avoid it. So from day one, I insisted that I clean the bathrooms; to this day, I've never let Leanne do that job. We've shared the cooking, laundry, and cleaning throughout our married years. The balance sometimes shifts, depending on who is working more outside the home.

> **BONUS TIP:** If you intend to get married—or even live on your own—learn how to clean and cook! Housework should be shared, so go into marriage expecting to do your share and more. It's a privilege to serve your spouse.

Good relationships require that we choose to put the needs of others ahead of our own. That's what Jesus meant when he said, "*Love your neighbor as yourself*" (Mark 12:31). Some people twist this and try to make it say, "Learn to love *yourself* so that you can love others better." That's pretty much exactly the opposite of what Jesus was saying.

Biblical love is the act of looking out for someone else's needs. It's an *action*, not just a *feeling*. "*God so <u>loved</u> the world, that he <u>gave</u> ...*" (John 3:16, emphasis added). Loving is giving and serving. It's doing the best for someone, choosing their needs above ours. We don't have to *feel* good about ourselves to put someone else's needs ahead of our own.

Jesus is saying, "In the same way you naturally look after your own needs, like feeding and clothing yourselves, look after the needs of those around you too." To love your neighbor *as yourself* means to look to *their* needs as you naturally look out for your own needs. Jesus was the perfect example of this, as shown in Philippians 2:3–8:

> *Do nothing from selfish ambition or conceit, but in humility count others more significant than yourselves. Let each of you look not only to his own interests, but also to the interests of others. Have this mind among yourselves, which is yours in Christ Jesus, who, though he was in the form of God, did not count equality with God a thing to be grasped, but emptied himself, by taking the form of a servant, being born in the likeness of men. And being found in human form, he humbled himself by becoming obedient to the point of death, even death on a cross.*

This passage helps define what it means to be a friend and a good companion.

1. Don't Be Selfish or Conceited

> *Do nothing from selfish ambition or conceit ...*

When you love to be the center of attention, many will enjoy your failures—especially with most people walking around with cameras on their phones! Countless people have even died attempting something foolish to gain a few "likes" on social media. Our society glorifies self-glorification.

So often I have displayed my insecurities by boasting or acting superior to others. I'm not sure which I fear more, success or failure. Failure at least teaches me and keeps me human; success can make me think far too much of myself. To relate well to others, we need to generously give credit and praise, remembering that everything worthwhile we accomplish is from God.

2. Be Humble

... but in humility ...

Humility is not so much thinking less of yourself than thinking about yourself—less. It's not humility to think of yourself as *worthless*; instead, humility takes the focus off yourself and considers others' needs and desires. Humble people don't talk about how awful they are; rather, they focus their interest on who *you* are, what *you* enjoy, and *your* current needs.

I wonder if anyone is naturally humble. The norm is to elevate ourselves above others. It takes a concerted effort to keep one's focus off ourselves and on someone else. I've known a few people like this. When you hear them pray, you realize they fully accept their frailties without self-pity. They are grateful to God and intent on pleasing him by serving others.

3. See Others as More Important than You

... count others more significant than yourselves.

It doesn't say, "consider others *equal* to you." Instead, we are to see their value and treat them as more important than we are. Sometimes I've caught myself thinking that someone is less valuable, especially in the work setting. I consciously need to remind myself that God made that person, loves them, and calls me to love them. He created them with the exact gifts and abilities required to fulfill an essential role in his world! We need to see people from God's perspective.

BONUS TIP: The quality of your life is generally based on the quality of your relationships—with God and people. You'll likely experience joy to the degree to which you have those relationships in order. The best thing we can do for ourselves is to invest in good relationships.

4. Look to the Interests of Others

Let each of you look not only to his own interests, but also to the interests of others.

This is the practical side of putting others first. Ask yourself, "What is best for this person in this situation? What can I do to help bring that about?" I would suggest three ways to make this real:

- **Encourage.** Be specific with your praise. Go out of your way—in speech, texts, emails, cards, and gifts—to help them see the good God sees in them.
- **Forgive.** Forgiveness acknowledges that we have been wronged yet releases others and ourselves from the harm and bitterness of not being forgiven. This should become natural when we understand the depths of forgiveness we need and have received through Jesus.
- **Serve.** Giving our time and talents to help others fulfills us in ways that never occur when we focus on our own needs. There is such joy in the simple decision to put others first and serve them, as Jesus did. We need to learn to be generous with our time.

5. Make Christ Your Example

Have this mind among yourselves, which is yours in Christ Jesus ...

The New Living Translation puts it this way, "*You must have the same attitude that Christ Jesus had.*" What was Jesus' attitude? Instead of coming to earth as the King, Creator, and Lord of all, he humbled himself, became a lowly human, served others, and obeyed his Father to the point of dying a gruesome death on a cross. The point is simple: if Jesus, being God, can serve and sacrifice himself for us, how much more should we follow his example and serve one another?

GETTING CLOSE TO GODLY PEOPLE

I already mentioned some godly young men who poured themselves into my life when I was in our church youth group. I believe that without their influence, I would have taken many wrong and destructive paths. Through that youth group, God gave me friends like Dale and others who wanted to follow God and helped me move in that same direction.

I've also had some terrible influences, especially when I was younger, people who often brought the worst out of me and got me into trouble. The more time I spent with them, the worse I acted, and if they were my only influences, I probably would have ended up living a life I would have been ashamed of.

I've heard it suggested that we are the average of the five people we spend the most time with. I find that incredibly sobering. Think about that. We naturally become like the people around us. And they become like us. Our companions are a major potential threat to our lives, yet they're also an incredible opportunity for us to be influenced positively and to influence others positively.

God's Word makes it clear how important choosing our companions is: "*Whoever walks with the wise becomes wise, but the companion of fools will suffer harm*" (Proverbs 13:20); "*Make no friendship with a man given to anger, nor go with a wrathful man, lest you learn his ways and entangle yourself in a snare*" (Proverbs 22:24–25); "*Do not be misled: 'Bad company corrupts good character'*" (1 Corinthians 15:33, NIV). Yet the Word also speaks of the benefits of good companions: "*Iron sharpens iron, and one man sharpens another*" (Proverbs 27:17). I have been so fortunate to have solid friendships with guys who have good character and who have sharpened me, even as I hopefully sharpened them.

I think of my Uncle Dave, whom I hadn't known growing up. He was a retired pastor who became a mentor to me as a young adult. For several years, he met with me regularly for lunch to talk about ministry, God's Word, and how to follow Jesus. The wisdom he shared and his living example made a huge difference in how I approached ministry and the Word of God.

Soon after Uncle Dave passed away, we started attending a church where every Saturday morning, a few mostly older and retired men would get together for prayer. I began to join them, and it was a great benefit to my spiritual life to get to know those godly men, pray with them, and hear their hearts breaking for the needs of the church and community.

> **BONUS TIP:** You will never regret spending time with older people who have walked the road you are on. However, you may regret *not* taking that time with them after they're gone.

Similarly, when we moved to Timberline Ranch, I found a wonderful group of pastors who met every Wednesday morning for prayer. I've had the privilege of their support and example week after week, year after year. We need to spend time with Jesus and with people who imitate Christ. The Apostle Paul wrote: "*Be imitators of me, as I am of Christ*" (1 Corinthians 11:1).

That's the kind of life I want—one that's so Christ-like that others can follow my example. If you spend time with godly people, you'll grow in that direction. Over time, you'll also become one who can influence others to take the right paths.

Find people who will help you become more like Christ. Force yourself upon them if necessary!

INFLUENCE

Influence plays an enormous role in our relationships and how we affect others and are affected by others. We tend to be like a thermometer or a thermostat in any given situation. A thermometer only tells us what the temperature around us *is*. It doesn't affect the temperature. So when the environment gets hot, the mercury rises, and we can see that it is hot in the room. When it gets cold, it goes down again.

We are like thermometers when we're influenced by people around us. There's not much we can do about it except choose to stay in that room or leave. If we remain, and the crowd we're with gets foolish, we, like thermometers, will tend to follow their lead. It would be better to find a different crowd at that time. However, if the crowd is wise, we'll also tend to follow that lead. That's a good crowd to stay with.

We can also learn to be more like thermostats. A thermostat doesn't just tell the temperature; it *determines* the temperature. If things are too cold, you turn up the thermostat, and the room gets warmer. If it's too hot, you simply turn it down.

To be a thermostat is to be a leader who influences the people around them. Rather than going with the crowd, they help determine where the crowd is going. Of course, this can be for good or bad. A wise leader is one who has developed good character from good influences in the past and can therefore influence others for good.

When I was in grade four, I thought my teacher, Mrs. Coulson, was fantastic. It was the 1970s, and she would have been classified as a hippy today. All I knew was that she was fun, creative, and enjoyable to learn from. Every week, she'd bring her guitar to class and teach us folksy songs, many of which I still remember, like "Blowing in the Wind," "Country Roads," and "Top of the World." We knew nothing about Bob Dylan, John Denver, or The Carpenters, but we belted out their songs because of Mrs. Coulson's influence.

However, I talked a lot in class and was a bit of a class clown. It drove my teachers crazy! We once had chicken eggs in an incubator, and the day came when they were supposed to hatch. We were all excited to see that happen, and my desk was right next to the incubator. But it took *forever*, and I was getting bored. So very quietly, I began to make little "cheeping" noises in the highest voice I could muster.

Apparently I succeeded, because the whole class jumped out of their seats and ran to the incubator to see the chickens hatching! I found it hilarious, but Mrs. Coulson gave me a look that said I had better start behaving better. Secretly, I think she thought I was pretty funny. Unfortunately, I was more amusing than I was smart because I tried it again a little later. This time, I only fooled a few kids and ended up in the hallway to think about my behavior.

> BONUS TIP: If you do something stupid, and someone gives you a free pass on it, take that as a hint not to do it again!

I don't remember if I was back in time to see the chickens hatch, but I didn't learn that lesson very well, and I continued to get into trouble throughout my elementary school years.

I was influential—a leader among my peers—but often not a good one. At least by the time I got to Bible school I was much better ... or so I thought. In my third year, I had a class with a teacher I wasn't particularly fond of. I have no idea why I didn't like her, but I kept my opinions to myself and did what I needed to get a decent grade. I focused on the assignments and put up with the class.

One day after class, our teacher asked me to stay behind. I had no idea why, and I was shocked when she said, "Craig, what is going on with you? Why do you have such a bad attitude in this class? Do you have any idea how much you're influencing everyone else?"

For once, I was speechless. How did she know I didn't enjoy her class when I disguised it so well? Here I was, training for Christian ministry, acting in a very ungodly way. I felt terrible. Of course, I apologized to her and promised to be better. From then on, I made sure I was positive in that class, despite how I felt about it. Once I adjusted my attitude, I also realized that the class wasn't so bad.

That incident made me realize the power of *influence* for good or evil. If I could *unconsciously* affect a group of students like that, then wow! That meant I needed to choose a good attitude wherever I went, no matter how I felt. If I was to be a leader and serve Jesus, I would need him to change my heart.

Leadership is truly all about *influence*, not merely authority. You don't need to be in a leadership position to influence—lead—those around you. Our influence comes from *who we are*, deep inside, our *character*. If our character is poor—if we're unwise—we will influence people to take harmful paths. However, if our character has been shaped by Jesus—if we have become wise—we will influence people to take good and righteous paths.

So choose to become a *good* influencer, a *good* leader. If you think that's not you, understand that it *can* be. Part of it is self-awareness and noticing how your comments and actions affect people around you. I managed to change when confronted with my bad attitude in that class. You can too.

The absolute best way to become a positive influencer is simply to *get to know Jesus*. We become like the people we spend the most time with, so spend lots of time with Jesus and people who love Jesus. He will change your heart and help you be the type of person others want to be around and imitate.

TEAMWORK

The West Coast Trail on Vancouver Island is one of the most beautiful places I have traveled. It's also one of the deadliest. It averages a death every two or three years, and dozens are evacuated from it every season due to injury or sickness. This I found out firsthand.

I was hired to help lead a trip for grade eleven students from a private school in Victoria. We would start on the north end of the Westcoast Trail and finish with canoeing inland on the Nitinat Triangle. The students had several different trips they could choose from, and this was one of the hardest. Two groups went on the trip: those who signed up for it and those assigned to it because they signed up late. Those assigned to it slogged through the rainforest while many of their friends spent a lovely week sailing on a tall ship.

> **BONUS TIP:** If you want the best options available in life, *don't procrastinate!*

Naturally, I was assigned the group of teens who didn't want to be there—all guys. Even better, most of them were in terrible shape for this kind of trip. Have I mentioned how important fitness is for the trail?

As we soon discovered, there's a lot of mud on the west coast of Vancouver Island. That might be due to the ridiculous amount of rain that falls there year-round. Much of our trip involved traipsing through the mud, and one canoe portage was almost two kilometers over a hill and through the mud. The student carrying a canoe with me sank into the mud to his knees and got stuck, and he couldn't even put the canoe down to get unstuck because the trees were too close around us! Thankfully, the only other people we saw that whole day came by at that exact moment, lifted the canoe from his shoulders, and helped him get out of the mud. I was so thankful for God's perfect timing! Unfortunately, the poor kid had to dig deep into the muck to find one of his shoes!

That portage should have taken about two to three hours, but it took our group *six hours*, and we were all exhausted by the end. I was so hot and tired, and I was about to suggest we all take a little dip in the water when I saw leeches lapping in the shallows. No thanks!

The next day, to avoid another lengthy portage, my co-leader (who had seniority) made the questionable decision to canoe down a creek that was supposed to be impassible. Sure enough, we came to a ten-to-twelve-foot-high jam of slippery logs. However, we noticed a small opening about six feet up that looked barely big enough to get a person or canoe through. It wasn't easy, but working together, we managed to get all five canoes, our gear, and every person through that hole. The creek on the other side was surprisingly clear of obstacles, and it was a leisurely paddle the rest of the way to the next lake.

On the final day, we had a very long lake to paddle to our pick-up point. We were all tired and filthy. A strong wind came up the lake from the ocean, so I had an idea. We pulled out a big tarp, tied it to some paddles, and had some boys hold them up at the front of the canoes. Everyone else held the canoes together, and I sat at the back, steering with a paddle. Working together like this, we sailed up the lake and made it to the end at least an hour earlier than expected.

It was a tough trip at times, but we made it and had a good time by working together. We began the trip as individuals but finished as a team. That sounds so cliché, but it's true! God has given us one another to work together, knowing that we are better working together than by ourselves.

INTERDEPENDENCE

From a young age, we're taught to grow from *dependence* to *independence*. Our society has elevated the value that we are our best selves when we don't need anyone else. However, God's way is *inter*dependence. Although it's healthy to be able to fend for oneself as needed, we're made for relationships and are truly at our best when contributing to and protected by our society. Ecclesiastes 4:9–12 reminds us of this need:

> *Two are better than one, because they have a good reward for their toil. For if they fall, one will lift up his fellow. But woe to him who is alone when he falls and has not another to lift him up! Again, if two lie together, they keep warm, but how can one keep warm alone? And though a man might prevail against one who is alone, two will withstand him—a threefold cord is not quickly broken.*

On the fourth day of our hiking and canoeing trip, we unexpectedly learned the lesson behind this principle. We received a radio call that an accident had occurred in one of the groups hiking the entire West Coast Trail, and one of the leaders had died. The name and circumstances were not being released, but we knew most of the other leaders and had trained with them at camp that spring, so we were very fearful of who it might be. We were suddenly reminded of how fragile life is, especially in the wilderness.

After our trip was over, some details of the tragedy were released. A woman in her forties—whom neither of us leaders knew—had left her group behind to scout the trail ahead. She evidently slipped on some rocks, fell into the ocean, and drowned. It was believed that her heavy backpack may have held her down and that she was unable to remove it. Her death was totally preventable, but no one was there to rescue her. The water wasn't deep, and she hadn't fallen far, but she was on the trail alone.

We *need* each other on this journey of life. We need to have each other's backs when difficulties come. We need to be able to celebrate together when we have successes and share the loads we bear. When we do, we can accomplish so much more! The strenuous journey can become a delightful adventure, even when we feel overwhelmed by the challenges or get stuck in the mud. God made us for community—to travel and to work together.

Don't walk your path alone. Find good people who can influence you well, learn to be a good friend, and influence others in the direction they should go.

CHOOSE YOUR OWN ADVENTURE

The Wise Path: I choose interdependence, sharing my life with others who love Jesus and can influence me in good directions.

The Foolish Path: I choose to succeed independently and build relationships with those who do not have my best interests at heart.

— Chapter Six —

WHEN YOU LOSE YOUR WAY

All we like sheep have gone astray;
we have turned—every one—to his own way;
and the Lord has laid on him the iniquity of us all.
~ Isaiah 53:6

When I was a young camper at Camp Qwanoes on Vancouver Island, I distinctly remember one hike that almost ended in disaster. The plan was to hike over Maple Mountain and down to a point on the ocean, where we would be met by the camp speedboat with everything we needed to stay there overnight. So we trudged our sleeping bags, clean clothes, and toothbrushes down to the dock and then took what felt like an arduous hike up that small mountain. Some of the route was a road, and the rest was a well-marked path. We were all tired at the top, but the view was lovely, and we enjoyed the cool breeze.

The most direct route from the top was to bushwhack down to the point rather than backtracking to a trail. Despite the lack of a path, the undergrowth was minimal, and we found our way down quite easily. Near the bottom, I heard someone ahead of me screaming in pain and panic. Suddenly, there was all sorts of movement as leaders came running towards us and told us not to go that way. So we diverted to the left and around where the screaming had occurred. Apparently we didn't go far enough, and I felt a sharp sting on my leg and then another.

We all began to panic a bit and ran in random directions. It probably took ten or fifteen minutes before the leaders could gather us all together again. Then we were told that one of the kids had stepped into a wasp nest and was stung multiple times—more than fifty, we found out later. The leaders did what First Aid they could and found some wild onions, which they told us to smear on the stings to help with the pain. Eventually, we found our way to our campsite. The boat met us and took the injured boy back to the camp, and the rest of us spent the night on the point. Many of us were sore, but it could have been much worse.

SINNING OR MISTAKING?

Leaving a worn path can be dangerous; however, it can be safe and fun with proper directional tools such as maps, compasses, and GPS. I often enjoy exploring beyond the well-trodden trails. In fact, as we'll look at in chapter ten, part of the joy of traveling with Jesus is the adventure of not knowing where he will lead you next. However, when we leave Jesus to go our *own* way, there are no benefits, only harm. He will often take us on unexpected paths, but the safest place is always *with him*.

There's a big difference between accidentally taking a wrong turn and abandoning the path on purpose to go our own way. This is similar to the difference between *making mistakes* and *sinning*. The difference between these is significant yet often confused by Christians. I've often heard Christians suggest that we need God to forgive us for our mistakes.

A *mistake* occurs when we act in ignorance, not intending to do wrong but doing something by accident, something unintended. For example, I was helping paint some signs for a youth event, and being a terrible painter, I accidentally painted beyond the lines someone had drawn. After a few repetitions of this failure, I was asked—nicely—to go help somewhere else. I was trying to paint well, but I was terrible at it.

By contrast, sin occurs when we either *do* what we know we should not do or *don't do* what we know we should do. At its very root, sin is an act of rebellion. When I get frustrated and speak unkindly to someone, that's sin. God has commanded me to love others, so I sin whenever I act unlovingly towards them. If I see that the dishes need to be washed, and I know I should do them but choose to do something fun, and then my wife has to do them, that is also sin. An unloving attitude and laziness are wrong; I should never refer to them as "mistakes."

> BONUS TIP: A lot of people talk about forgiving *themselves*. While it's true that we also hurt ourselves

> when we sin, only God can forgive us. Simply telling
> ourselves that what we did was okay does not remove
> our guilt. However, once we have received forgiveness,
> we must learn to see ourselves as God sees us—loved,
> worthy, and forgiven!

Sometimes sins and mistakes can look very similar. Is it a sin or mistake if a child knocks over a glass of milk at dinner? Well, it depends. If their parent told them to stop waving their hands around, and they did anyway, thus spilling their milk, that's sin. God's Word says for children to obey their parents. However, if they simply reached for something and knocked it over, that's probably just a mistake, and they merely need to learn to be more careful.

I often wonder: Did Jesus make mistakes? Did he ever accidentally cut a board too short, trip over a stone, or drop a jar on the floor? If we are to affirm his full *humanity*—as the Bible does—then we would have to say that yes, Jesus made mistakes! But did He ever lust after a woman, disobey his parents, or gossip about someone? Again, if we affirm his full *divinity*—as the Bible does—we know he was tempted but sinless. But I'll bet his siblings loved to see him make mistakes!

SIN ROCKS

The summer after I graduated from high school, I couldn't afford to go directly to college, so I decided to work for a year. This also meant I could volunteer my time for the summer. Our local Youth for Christ group was running a missions trip to central California in the Grasslands area for the first three weeks of July, and I decided to go if I could. As mentioned earlier, God provided my exact financial needs, and I was thrilled, especially since some of my friends were going.

We stayed and worked at a ranch that ran programs for troubled teens. We constructed an outdoor chapel area with benches and did a lot of cleaning and repairing. On a few days off, we went sightseeing and got to go for a swim in the beautiful Yuba River, which was a lot of fun.

At the camp, there were bats in the washrooms, which made it challenging to brush your teeth while dancing around, trying to avoid them. The boys' and girls' sides were joined by a middle wall, and sometimes the girls would be silly and knock on their side of the wall. Once when they did this, I went up to the wall and smacked it hard, just once, with both hands. The sound was something like this: *BAM! ... **BOOM!!!***

When I hit the wall, I caused a fluorescent light tube to fall from the ceiling and shatter about a foot behind me. I didn't see it fall, and it startled me half to death! I hadn't done anything sinful—there was no rule about hitting the wall—but my mistake in judgment caused a mess, and I had to clean it up. Mistakes often require apologizing and then fixing what has been done wrong.

> **BONUS TIP:** When visiting another part of the world, don't assume anything is up to the same building codes you're used to. Much construction in other parts of the world is done to different standards, especially in third-world countries, but potentially anywhere you visit.

It was a great trip, but I had a sharp disagreement with one of the leaders. My attitude suffered, and I allowed my frustrations with him to affect my ability to serve. I thought I was standing up for others who felt similarly, but I was rebelling against the God-given leadership of our missions team. It was sin, and I had to repent and seek forgiveness from the leader and the rest of the team.

Probably as a punishment for my less-than-stellar attitude, I was given the solo job of trying to remove a rock from a dirt road. It was just me, a shovel, and the one-hundred-degree furnace they call summer. The stone was sticking up just high enough to occasionally scrape the underside of cars that came through, so it was my job to make things safer. The rock's surface was maybe four inches by about three inches, so I figured it shouldn't be too hard to dig out.

However, the road was hard-packed dirt or clay, and there was no way I could dig the rock out with a shovel, so I got a pickaxe and gradually broke the hard ground around it. The trouble was, the more I dug around the rock, the bigger it got. So I tried a different approach, attempting to break the rock with the pickaxe, but to no avail. Figuring I needed more power, I got a sledgehammer. I smacked away at it, occasionally chipping off small fragments, which sometimes pinged painfully off my bare legs. Apparently, granite is stronger than I am!

I soon gave up on that approach and returned to digging around it. I dug. And I dug. But the farther I dug down, the wider the rock got! I'm not a complete fool, so I eventually realized that this was not a stone or even a boulder but part of the *hillside*. I determined it would be better to build up the road *over* the top of this rock or build a road *around* it, because this thing was not going anywhere!

I wish I knew a cool Hebrew word that means "The Rock of My Defeat." Then I would name it, and it would become famous. That rock was a lot bigger and tougher than I was.

Reflecting on this experience later, I realized that my sins are like that rock. Mostly I try to keep my bad attitudes hidden under the surface, but occasionally they pop up and cause a problem, like that rock hitting someone's muffler or me getting frustrated with my leader. However, I can't remove my sins, no matter how hard I try. They're too big for me. Unless God forgives me and removes my sins, they remain deeply embedded in me. Praise God for forgiveness in Jesus!

WHY IS SIN SINFUL?

As a child, I always found it frustrating to ask an adult why I couldn't do something. They invariably said something like, "Because I said so." But *why* did you say so? Growing up in the church, it was similar with sin. I was told that certain actions and attitudes were wrong because God says so in the Bible. But *why*? It seemed so random.

Yet God's commands are not arbitrary in the least. They're based on *who God is*. Every command is based on the character of God. He is the standard of perfection, and when we obey him, we live the best life we can. We're to tell the truth because he is True. We're to be faithful in marriages and relationships because he is Faithful. We must not murder because he is Life. The greatest commands, Jesus said, are to love God and love other people—because God is Love!

When we sin, either by what we do or what we fail to do, we turn away from the absolute best God has for us. We miss out on the life we're designed to live and enjoy. Worst of all, we begin to find enjoyment in our sins and start to doubt that there's anything better. Essentially, we turn our backs on God and go our own ways.

Often as Christians we sin and then ask for forgiveness, knowing we want to return to it again. And again. Maybe we even promise ourselves to avoid it in the future. But we can never keep those promises. Perhaps we're not entirely convinced that sin is even *bad*. Jesus paid for it, so why not enjoy it? How bad can it be if all we need to do is ask for forgiveness every time?

The Apostle Paul takes on that argument in Romans 5 and 6. God's grace came because of sin, so why not sin more so that his grace increases even more? *"What shall we say then? Are we to continue in sin that grace may abound? By no means! How can we who died to sin still live in it?"* (Romans 6:1–2).

We don't understand how bad sin is because we fail to grasp how *holy* God is. We can't even begin to comprehend how far above us God's perfection exists in his character, beauty, righteousness, or power. He is described in 1 Timothy 6:15–16 as:

> … *he who is the blessed and only Sovereign, the King of kings and Lord of lords, who alone has immortality, who dwells in unapproachable light, whom no one has ever seen or can see. To him be honor and eternal dominion. Amen.*

This is the God who willingly was tortured and crucified on the cross to pay for our sins, yet we turn and thumb our nose at him in rebellion.

HOW GOD DESCRIBES SIN

Sin is why many will spend eternity in hell, a place described as a lake of fire, completely distanced from the presence and goodness of God. That sounds so harsh. Isn't God loving? Doesn't he just kind of ignore our little rebelliousness, like a good old uncle who may chide us gently but loves us too much to bother about the "little things"? Here's how God describes the effects of sin:

Sin leads to death—"*Therefore, just as sin came into the world through one man, and death through sin, and so death spread to all men because all sinned …*" (Romans 5:12); "*For the wages of sin is death …*" (Romans 6:23a).

Sin causes blindness—"*But whoever hates his brother is in the darkness and walks in the darkness, and does not know where he is going, because the darkness has blinded his eyes*" (1 John 2:11).

Sin brings slavery—"*Jesus answered them, 'Truly, truly, I say to you, everyone who practices sin is a slave to sin*" (John 8:34).

Sin produces God's wrath—"*For the wrath of God is revealed from heaven against all ungodliness and unrighteousness of men, who by their unrighteousness suppress the truth*" (Romans 1:18).

Sin causes eternal separation from God—"*Behold, the Lord's hand is not shortened, that it cannot save, or his ear dull, that it cannot hear; but your iniquities have made a separation between you and your God, and your sins have hidden his face from you so that he does not hear*" (Isaiah 59:1–2).

Sin brings judgment—"*For if we go on sinning deliberately after receiving the knowledge of the truth, there no longer remains a sacrifice for sins, but a fearful expectation of judgment, and a fury of fire that will consume the adversaries*" (Hebrews 10:26–27).

GETTING OFF-TRACK IS EASY

A few years ago, I took my family for a short hike in Minnekhada Park near Vancouver. Just as we left the parking lot, three young adults came running up the path towards us with terror in their eyes.

"There's a bear!" they told us, breathless from their run. Apparently, they didn't know that running from a bear was foolish, but I found out where they saw the bear so we could avoid that area. I quickly looked at the map and determined a route to bypass the danger.

However, I accidentally made a wrong turn, taking us exactly where I was trying to avoid! Leanne and I were ahead of our kids, and suddenly I heard a movement behind me, and there was the bear in the bushes, just six feet from my daughter! The bear took off into the bushes, but Lorelle was understandably somewhat shaken by the encounter. To her credit, she gave barely a shriek, and she continued the hike, despite the shock.

For my part, I felt terrible! It was an awful mistake. I apologized profusely, looked at a map, and figured out where I'd gone wrong. At an unusual double intersection, I should have turned left instead of a slight right and *then* left. That one little mistake could have had enormous consequences. Fortunately, the rest of the hike was bear-free and enjoyable, but I was amazed at how easily I got off-track despite knowing where I wanted to go.

> BONUS TIP: Be prepared for any wild animal you might encounter when hiking, and do your best to give them lots of room. This includes wildlife you see along the highway! Don't try to get close to take a photo, like many have done disastrously with bison in Yellowstone Park …

Even with good intentions, we often wander off the path. Even when we know the right direction, we sometimes miss it. Do you ever get tired of messing up? How do we avoid that constant cycle of needing to find the path again? One of my favorite verses is 1 John 1:9: "*If we confess our sins, he is faithful and just to forgive us our sins and to cleanse us from all unrighteousness.*"

When we sin, the first step is undoubtedly repentance, turning *away* from sin and *to* God. We must confess our sins, agreeing with God that our sin is wrong and his way is right. God not only forgives us—he cleans us up!

Yet even after I've received forgiveness and cleansing, I wander off the path again. I used to think I'd be better if I tried harder, but that isn't the case. Then I figured that I'd sin less if I just grew spiritually. That's probably true. However, the closer we get to God and see sin as he does, the more sensitive we become to our sins. Sins we wouldn't have noticed before now become evident.

IS THERE HOPE?

This may be the most critical question we ask. Sin is so powerful, so devastating, so controlling. Is there a path that leads to freedom? The Apostle Paul, believing himself to be the evilest of all sinners for how he pursued and murdered followers of Jesus, also wrestled with this:

> *For I know that nothing good dwells in me, that is, in my flesh. For I have the desire to do what is right, but not the ability to carry it out. For I do not do the good I want, but the evil I do not want is what I keep on doing . . . Wretched man that I am! Who will deliver me from this body of death?* (Romans 7:18–19, 24)

What a mess sin has brought to our lives! If Paul stopped right there, if there was nothing to be done about sin, we would genuinely be in a hopeless position. However, he continued: *"Thanks be to God through Jesus Christ our Lord! … There is therefore now no condemnation for those who are in Christ Jesus"* (Romans 7:25, 8:1).

No condemnation! There is no guilt remaining for those who have been redeemed by Jesus! There is complete forgiveness and a path back. The highway to hell has an exit ramp. God doesn't simply forgive us; he picks us up, cleans us off, and welcomes us as his own children. Look at what the rest of Romans 8 tells us about our new situation if we trust in Jesus:

- No longer slaves but free (8:2)
- Indwelt by God (8:9, 23)
- Children of God (8:14–16)
- Adopted by God (8:15)
- Heirs of God alongside Jesus (8:17)
- Saved (8:24)
- Chosen and called by God (8:28–30)
- Justified (8:33)
- Conquerors (8:37)
- Inseparable from God's love (8:38–39)

Is there hope? Absolutely! The path to freedom from sin is found in a relationship with God through Jesus Christ.

THE LOST CAN BE FOUND!

One of my favorite chapters in the Bible is Luke 15. It includes stories of the lost sheep, the lost coin, and the lost (or *prodigal*) son. They are beautiful reminders of God's love and forgiveness.

Jesus had been drawing large crowds, especially attracting the lowest rungs of society, such as tax collectors (seen by the Jews as traitors working for Rome), prostitutes, and criminals—people who *knew* they were sinners. At the end of Luke 14, Jesus says, "*He who has ears, let him hear*" (v. 35b). In other words, listen carefully, and then wisely do what I tell you. Luke says that these sinners "*were all drawing near to hear him*" (15:1). They were listening!

Contrasted with them were the religious leaders. They also gathered around Jesus, not so much to *hear* but to *criticize*. In 15:2, Luke writes that they were grumbling about Jesus, saying, "*This man receives sinners and eats with them.*" In other words, Jesus couldn't possibly be a righteous rabbi if he hung around with sinners.

In response, Jesus gives these three parables to demonstrate the value of the sinners gathered around him. A shepherd loses one of his hundred sheep. He leaves the rest where they are safe and then does whatever it takes to safely get that sheep back home. This may have taken several days of searching through the hills, and the sheep, paralyzed with fear, would likely have needed to be carried all the way back. When he finally returns the sheep, the shepherd is so happy that he throws a big party. Jesus concludes the story by saying, *"Just so, I tell you, there will be more joy in heaven over one sinner who repents than over ninety-nine righteous persons who need no repentance"* (15:7).

It seems that the religious leaders were unimpressed—after all, what was a sheep to them? So Jesus gives them another story about something they could better relate to: money. A woman loses a valuable coin, one of ten she owns. She lights a lamp in that dark house with a dirt floor and sweeps everywhere to find it. And when she finds it, she rejoices and has a big party. Again, Jesus concludes the parable by saying, *"Just so, I tell you, there is joy before the angels of God over one sinner who repents"* (15:10).

Undoubtedly, the religious leaders understood Jesus' point about the value of these "sinners" and their need to repent, but they were unmoved. So Jesus presses on with something they would see as immeasurably more valuable than a sheep or coin—a son. You can read this fantastic story in Luke 15:11–32, but the gist of it is that a younger son takes his inheritance early—a terrible insult to his family—and goes far away to a pagan nation. If that wasn't bad enough, he wastes the entire inheritance on sinful, *extravagant* living (from which we get the word *prodigal*). He runs out of money, ends up feeding pigs for employment, and begins to starve to death.

This son ends up where much of Jesus' crowd was right then. Hopeless. Lost. Far from home. Most of the religious leaders would have believed he got what he deserved.

However, it doesn't end there! The son finally comes to his senses, turns back home, and finds his father not only waiting for him but *running* towards him with open arms! For a man to run was considered shameful in that culture. Yet in his love for his son, the father cared not. The son repents and is reinstated as a son with full rights and privileges. And, of course, the father throws a huge party! Why? Because his lost son had come home.

BONUS TIP: There are so many great reasons to
celebrate. We don't have to wait for a birthday or special
event. Why not just throw a party for someone you love
or even for some minor achievement? God loves parties,
and he loves to see us enjoying life!

Clearly, Jesus is illustrating to the sinners listening that there *is* a
way back home, that their heavenly Father desperately wants them to
repent and return to him. The path home begins with recognizing we
are lost and then turning around and heading back to God. This is what
repentance is all about—turning from our sins, turning to God, and
finding him waiting for us with open arms.

Another time when Jesus was asked by the religious leaders as to
why he hung out with sinners, he replied, "*Those who are well have no
need of a physician, but those who are sick. I have not come to call the
righteous but sinners to repentance*" (Luke 5:31–32).

While we have life and breath, there is a way home, a path that
leads to forgiveness and new life. You can never go so far away that God
the Father is not watching down the road, waiting for you to return to
him. Like the shepherd, he has done whatever it took to bring you back.
Like the woman who lost a coin, he values you greatly. Like a father, he
desperately loves you.

The story of the lost son doesn't end with his return; it ends with
a very unexpected turn. Jesus tells them about an older son, who
represents the religious leaders. In his arrogance and lack of forgiveness,
this son despises his brother for his sinful behavior. He's unwilling to
come inside for the party, even with his father begging him to do so. He
self-righteously disowns his brother, and he doesn't recognize his own
need for the father.

Sadly, at the end of the story, despite the father's invitation to
come and join the party, the older brother *still has not come home*. He
remains outside, refusing to repent. Like these religious leaders, he's too
concerned about the sins of others to see his own failings. And without
acknowledging his own sins, his relationship with the father cannot be
repaired.

The lost are only a moment of repentance away from the path back home. The way back is never easy, but God loves you more than you can imagine and is ready to welcome you home—today!

GETTING BACK ON THE PATH

So how do we stop sinning? What can I do to avoid sin and live a godlier life? The key that so many of us miss is *accountability*. It's connected to the interdependence we looked at in chapter five.

In Hebrews 10, the writer warns about God's judgment if we continue to sin deliberately, but he precedes it with this important advice:

> *[L]et us* draw near *with a true heart in full assurance of faith, with our hearts sprinkled clean from an evil conscience and our bodies washed with pure water. Let us* hold fast *the confession of our hope without wavering, for he who promised is faithful. And let us consider how to* stir up one another *to love and good works, not neglecting to meet together, as is the habit of some, but* encouraging one another, *and all the more as you see the Day drawing near.* (Hebrews 10:22–25, emphasis added)

Specifically, then, if we're to avoid the continuous cycle of sin, we need to:

- Draw near to God (v. 22)
- Hold fast to the confession of our hope (v. 23)
- Help each other live right (v. 24)
- Meet regularly with other believers (v. 25)
- Encourage one another (v. 25)

How do we "draw near" to God? We'll talk more about this in the next chapter, but it has a lot to do with the intentionality of spending time with God in prayer, fasting, meditating on his Word, and serving him.

Instead of sinning, we must "*hold fast to the confession of our hope.*" In other words, don't give up on the one we trusted to begin with. He is faithful, and his promises to keep us in his love never fail! A verse that is very important to me is Philippians 1:6: "*And I am sure of this, that he who began a good work in you will bring it to completion at the day of Jesus Christ.*" Although we may sometimes fail and turn our back on him, our salvation depends on *him*, not on us.

The final three points in this passage are all about living in *community* with other believers: "*Stir up one another to love and good works.*" In other words, stimulate each other to live right. "*Not neglecting to meet together*" refers to coming together for worship and using our gifts to build one another up. Finally, "*encouraging one another*" is (in context) about reminding one another that Jesus is coming back. Our temporary struggles are worthwhile!

If we're serious about avoiding sin and living for God, we must help one another. Look at James 5:13–16:

> *Is anyone among you suffering? Let him pray. Is anyone cheerful? Let him sing praise. Is anyone among you sick? Let him call for the elders of the church, and let them pray over him, anointing him with oil in the name of the Lord. And the prayer of faith will save the one who is sick, and the Lord will raise him up. And if he has committed sins, he will be forgiven. Therefore, confess your sins to one another and pray for one another, that you may be healed. The prayer of a righteous person has great power as it is working.*

We often focus on individual confession, but here James is saying we need to confess our sins *to one another* and pray *for one another* for the forgiveness of our sins.

I wonder if the biggest problem in the church today is that we simply don't obey God's Word in this. Could it be that we are taught, perhaps unintentionally, that our private sins are our own personal problems and have no effect on anyone else? What if we obeyed and lived in community in such a way that we stopped hiding our sins from each other but openly confessed them and helped one another stay on the path?

Living in authentic Christian community is the key to getting back on the path. As we'll see in the next chapter, it's also a key to *staying* on the path.

We don't have to keep going back to the same sins. Second Timothy 3:16–17 tells us how to get back and stay on the path as we submit to his Word: *"All Scripture is breathed out by God and profitable for <u>teaching</u>, for <u>reproof</u>, for <u>correction</u>, and for <u>training in righteousness</u>, that the man of God may be complete, equipped for every good work"* (emphasis added).

Notice four things here about the profitability of submitting to God's Word:

- **Teaching**—God's Word shows us which paths to take.
- **Reproof**—God's Word shows us where we got off the path.
- **Correction**—God's Word shows us how to get back on the path.
- **Training in Righteousness**—God's Word shows us how to continue down the right paths.

As we are taught and trained in righteousness, we will be *"complete, equipped for every good work."* In other words, whereas a cycle of sinning makes us ineffective for God, a cycle of holding fast to God's Word makes us effective for him. And that's our goal—to bring glory to God by loving and obeying him.

THE UPSIDE TO FAILURE

Albert Einstein has been credited with saying: "Anyone who has never made a mistake has never tried anything new."[4] That is so true! The only way to accomplish something is to put yourself in a position where you might fail.

I once worked in a place that had a fleet of vehicles. When we drove one, we were responsible for checking it over and promptly reporting any maintenance issues. We were also instructed to add oil if it was needed.

One day, a young lady on staff came inside and asked for a piece of paper. One of my coworkers found some for her and thought nothing of it. Not long afterward, he could hear her making loud noises of anguish and frustration. When he went to see the problem, he noticed she had fresh oil all over her hands.

"This isn't working!" she screamed in frustration as he approached.

"What are you trying to do?" he asked carefully.

"I'm trying to top up the oil! It keeps coming back out!"

"Ah ... I see," he replied. "Um, can I maybe show you a better way to do that?"

She had checked the oil via the dipstick, as she had been shown to do. It was low, so she figured she needed to add oil. Unfortunately, she didn't know where the oil should be added, so she tried to pour it down the dipstick! She made a funnel from a piece of paper, but it wasn't working as well as she'd hoped.

We can laugh at her failure—admittedly, we did—but I applaud her effort. Many people in her situation would have ignored the low oil and left the problem for the following driver to solve. Instead, she found a creative—albeit technically flawed—solution and did her best. She undoubtedly learned from it and knew where to add oil correctly in the future.

Why are most people so afraid to fail? Is it so important that we get everything right on the first try?

A few years ago, I learned a new expression: *fail forward*. I love that! The idea is that every time we make a mistake, we learn and grow from it. Failure becomes a launching pad to future success.

When my wife was selling Usborne kids' books a number of years ago, she was trying to find people to host book parties where she could present the books. One of the challenges the publishing company gave those selling the books was to see how many "no" answers they could get. They knew that if they got enough people saying "no," some would say "yes." This encouraged Leanne to be less nervous about asking people, knowing that getting negative responses was part of eventually getting positive ones.

I love Thomas Edison's quote after unsuccessfully attempting to invent a lightbulb for years: "I have not failed. I've just found 10,000 ways that won't work."[5]

When our failure isn't a moral failure (i.e., it isn't sin), our best response is to keep trying different ways to achieve our objective. Get back up and try again. God has given you talents and good works to accomplish, so never let a setback end your efforts. Rejoice that you have another chance to succeed!

DON'T BE AFRAID OF DOUBTS

Something that can easily keep us from getting back on the path is our doubts—our difficulties in believing that God is faithful or that he even exists. It's essential to understand that *doubting is okay*, at least to a point.

Too many Christians are even more afraid to express their doubts than admit their sins. What would people think of me if they knew _____? Fill in the blank. That you're a sinner? Yes, they know that! That you have doubts? Yes, they know that too, because they also have doubts.

I love the example of the Apostle Thomas. Picture the scene: Jesus died a horrendous death on the cross, and the disciples scattered, fearing that they might be associated with Jesus and executed as well. Everything they believed about Jesus had been shattered. Jesus had said he would rise from the dead, but they simply couldn't understand or believe that.

Then there were rumors. Some women said the tomb was empty. Some men said they met him on the road. And now other disciples had apparently seen him. He appeared to a big group of them! Still, Thomas questioned the validity of the stories.

> *Now Thomas … was not with the disciples when Jesus came. So the other disciples told him, "We have seen the Lord!" But he said to them, "Unless I see the nail marks in his hands and put my finger where the nails were, and put my hand into his side, I will not believe." (John 20:24–25, NIV)*

Thomas' hopes had been shattered. I grew up reading this story thinking Thomas was wrong or even sinful to doubt, but as I look at it today, I think I understand his reluctance to believe. Why should he trust the tales of the other disciples? They'd been wrong so many times! Why would he simply believe them about such an important detail? After all, if Jesus rose from the dead, that changed everything!

We should doubt. We should question. We should make sure that what we believe is true. Our eternal destinies depend upon it, so why would we simply believe what someone tells us or teaches us without looking into it carefully? I love what the Bereans did with the gospel message when Paul came to them: "*Now these Jews were more noble than those in Thessalonica; they received the word with all eagerness, examining the Scriptures daily to see if these things were so. Many of them therefore believed …*" (Acts 17:11–12a).

Notice that their belief only took place *after* they had studied the scriptures to ensure that what Paul said lined up with the prophecies in the Old Testament—the only scriptures they had at that time. And when they saw the truth revealed, they ended their doubts and followed Jesus wholeheartedly. We see the same with Thomas.

> *A week later his disciples were in the house again, and Thomas was with them. Though the doors were locked, Jesus came and stood among them and said, "Peace be with you!" Then he said to Thomas, "Put your finger here; see my hands. Reach out your hand and put it into my side. Stop doubting and believe." Thomas said to him, "My Lord and my God!" Then Jesus told him, "Because you have seen me, you have believed; blessed are those who have not seen and yet have believed."* (John 20:26–29, NIV)

It's not just *okay* to doubt; it's *crucial* to scrutinize everything we're told, especially from anyone who purports to teach spiritual truth. To doubt honorably isn't to criticize everything but to carefully examine things to see if they are wisdom or folly. Once we're convinced, we act on that truth.

BONUS TIP: Please scrutinize everything I'm telling you in this book! None of my education, experiences, or good intentions make me an expert or necessarily correct. If at any point my writing doesn't truly represent God's Word, please disregard it!

Faith is not an exercise of throwing away what we know and "believing anyway." It is never blind. It's always based on the building blocks of what we already know to be true. I get on an airplane and trust the pilot to take me safely to my destination based on the fact of the airline's record and the general safety of air travel. However, faith is only as good as the object of our faith, and it's true that from time to time, a plane will crash.

Yet when we put our faith in the God of the universe, it's a 100 percent thing. He will *never* fail you; he will *never* forsake you. Don't take my word for it—investigate it yourself! He promised his people in Jeremiah 29:13, "*You will seek me and find me when you seek me with all your heart*" (NIV).

Returning to the path means seeking God with all our hearts, trusting his Word, and living in authentic Christian community. It means allowing ourselves to be vulnerable with others and with God. People will fail us, but God never will. Will you trust him today?

CHOOSE YOUR OWN ADVENTURE

The Wise Path: I choose to turn back to my loving Father whenever I find myself on the wrong path, submitting to his rule in my life, and continuously seeking the Truth in him.

The Foolish Path: I choose to ignore God's warnings and continue down paths that enslave me now and lead to judgment in the life to come.

— Chapter Seven —
STAYING ON THE PATH

I will instruct you and teach you in the way you should go;
I will counsel you with my eye upon you.
~ Psalm 32:8

M any years after that somewhat disastrous hike over Maple Mountain, I was working my summers at Camp Qwanoes, and an overnight trip was planned for the point. However, the arduous trek over the mountain was replaced with a simple stroll along a two-kilometer path. I suppose kids had become a little less hardy over the intervening years. That's my theory, anyway.

Soon after we arrived, the camp boat came with all the gear, and we had all the boys form a giant chain to get everything up to the plateau where we were camping. We made a fire, got some roasting sticks, and consumed hot dogs, chips, and juice boxes. A few of the staff came later in a canoe after they were done their duties back at camp.

As night approached, we unpacked some tarps for groundsheets, and all eighty or so of us found places to throw our sleeping bags and pillows. Eventually, everyone fell asleep ... only to be awakened at about 2:00 a.m. by a torrential downpour. Everyone scurried to get under the tarp, which became a hot mess. I quickly discovered that I was allergic to the grass and dust beneath, and I started wheezing, so I got out and found a tree to stand under.

In the meantime, there was a minor medical emergency, and our First Aider was suddenly busy helping a camper. We had no adequate way to get the camper back to the camp in the dark or to contact the camp, so we decided to send a couple of people back to get help. I offered to go, since I wasn't going to sleep any more that night, and we decided it would be a lot easier to canoe back than to try to find our way through the dark forest. My friend Wes joined me, and we grabbed a canoe, lifejackets, paddles, and flashlights.

Boating at night in the pitch dark isn't usually wise. Even with flashlights, you have little sense of direction, and it would be easy to go the wrong direction. We decided to attempt it because a solitary light shone from the camp lodge on a hill, and we could see it the whole way. We just had to head towards the light. I was in the back of the canoe, where most of the steering takes place. As long as I kept my eyes on that light and kept it in front of us, we went straight towards the camp. However, sometimes we got talking, and I took my eyes off it. Sure enough, we started heading off track and had to correct our course.

We would have been in serious trouble had that light gone out! Fortunately, it stayed bright, and we made it to the camp and arranged for a boat to head out as soon as it got light.

JESUS IS THE LIGHT

In John 8:12, Jesus said, *"I am the light of the world. Whoever follows me will not walk in darkness, but will have the light of life."* If we want to know where we're going in life—if we're going to stay on the right path—we need to follow Jesus closely. When we do, we also become lights to help others find their way to Jesus, as he explained in Matthew 5:14–16:

> *You are the light of the world. A city set on a hill cannot be hidden. Nor do people light a lamp and put it under a basket, but on a stand, and it gives light to all in the house. In the same way, let your light shine before others, so that they may see your good works and give glory to your Father who is in heaven.*

Like canoeing in the dark, the key is to keep our eyes on that Light. If we do, we will stay far from sin and danger, and we can lead others in the way they should go. Jesus must be the focus of our lives if we want to stay on course.

PETER

One of Jesus' closest friends and followers was a fisherman named Peter. He was an "act first, think later" kind of guy, but he was also very dedicated to Jesus and desperately wanted to follow him. One day the disciples were in a boat, fighting against a strong headwind late at night, when Jesus came walking towards them—on the water! They were terrified, thinking it was a ghost, but Jesus called out to them and assured them it was he.

Peter logically concluded—if he thought at all before acting—that if Jesus could walk on water, he could also enable Peter to walk on water. Of course!

> *And Peter answered him, "Lord, if it is you, command me to come to you on the water." He said, "Come." So Peter got out of the boat and walked on the water and came to Jesus. But when he saw the wind, he was afraid, and beginning to sink he cried out, "Lord, save me." Jesus immediately reached out his hand and took hold of him, saying to him, "O you of little faith, why did you doubt?" And when they got into the boat, the wind ceased. And those in the boat worshiped him, saying, "Truly you are the Son of God." (Matthew 14:28–33)*

This story should amaze and surprise us on so many levels. But I want to highlight this: Peter put his faith in Jesus and trusted him enough to get out of the boat—a seemingly crazy thing to do—and *walked on water* until he took his eyes off Jesus. As soon as he looked at the storm around him, he began to sink.

We may think, *Peter! You just had to trust Jesus and keep your focus on him!* Honestly, I would have probably been like the other eleven disciples who stayed in the boat. It's no great accomplishment to drown for Jesus. Yet I love that Peter didn't just jump out of the boat. He first made sure that it was Jesus' *will* that Peter walk on the water. Once Jesus said, "Come," Peter knew he would be safe doing the seemingly impossible.

> BONUS TIP: Risking everything for Jesus is great—if it's
> truly for Jesus. Be careful that the risk you take is for *his*
> glory, not your own.

Keeping our eyes on Jesus means ensuring that our faith is in him, following his will daily, and not giving in to worrying about the storms around us and the voices telling us that what we're doing is impossible. According to John 14:12–14, God will empower those with faith to do even greater works than Jesus did!

> *Truly, truly, I say to you, whoever believes in me will also do the works that I do; and greater works than these will he do, because I am going to the Father. Whatever you ask in my name, this I will do, that the Father may be glorified in the Son. If you ask me anything in my name, I will do it.*

DIFFICULT TRAILS

During the second spring of COVID-19, some of the wooded trails on our camp property rapidly became overgrown without constant use. Not knowing this, my son, Ben, and I decided to go for a hike to access trails far beyond our property.

The closest trails had been used a bit, and they were fine, but the farther we went, the more grown-in they were. Although I thought I knew the trails well, we surprisingly missed a major turnoff and had to retrace our steps to find it. It was completely covered with new growth and hidden from view. Once I figured out where the trail was, it was easier for a while. Although I still couldn't see the path, my feet could *feel* where it was, so I trusted my feet. However, it got worse the farther we went, and from time to time, I had to turn around and walk backward to push my way through the thick growth.

Eventually, we got to a place where a tangle of bushes had grown over so much that I could no longer even push my way through. Worst of all, my legs and arms were getting all cut up by the branches. Finally finding a boulder to scramble over, we broke out to a clearing under some power lines. What a relief! After a few wrong turns, we eventually found a way to connect to the trail we were looking for, and we felt like we had accomplished something. Those cuts and scrapes, however, lasted for several days.

Sometimes life—the trail—feels a whole lot harder than it should be. We get battered by all the difficulties we face, and it can seem like there's no way forward. We're tempted to give up or take a different path. That's when we most need to double down and press on. That's when we need to trust that God knows where he's taking us.

MAKING A CHANGE

How do we *stay* on the right track? What gives us the strength and perseverance to keep going when the trail is narrow and difficult? Ephesians 4 gives us some good insight into this. After explaining how God gives spiritual gifts to his Church for building one another up, Paul reminds them:

> ... *you must no longer walk as the Gentiles do, in the futility of their minds. They are darkened in their understanding, alienated from the life of God because of the ignorance that is in them, due to their hardness of heart. They have become callous and have given themselves up to sensuality, greedy to practice every kind of impurity.* (Ephesians 4:17b–19)

Look at the words he uses here:

- "futility of their minds"
- "darkened in their understanding"
- "ignorant"
- "hardness of heart"
- "callous"

As we discussed in chapter two, there is a spiritual battle for our minds, because how we think is how we act. However, the reverse is also true—how we act dramatically affects our thinking. Those who have not received new life through Jesus—the "Gentiles"—are alienated from the life that is in God, because the longer they resist him, the harder their hearts get. Thus, they live sensual, impure lives. This lifestyle reinforces their wrong thinking, leading them to further ungodly actions, which leads them farther away from God.

This is what it means to be slaves to sin—becoming captive to this way of thinking and acting. There is no way out! The only escape from this prison is if Jesus steps in, removes our chains, and leads us out. When we choose to follow him instead of the futility of this world's ways, he gives us new life and a new identity, and he begins to change our hearts and ways of thinking. He sets us on a new path.

> BONUS TIP: We are multifaceted people, and our identity is not fundamentally based on our sexual preferences or gender. Rather, as believers, our identity is as children of the Most High God, those redeemed and set free by Jesus so that all aspects of our lives would come under his Lordship.

Paul shows the way forward in the following verses:

> But that is not the way you learned Christ!—assuming that you have heard about him and were taught in him, as the truth is in Jesus, to put off your old self, which belongs to your former manner of life and is corrupt through deceitful desires, and to be renewed in the spirit of your minds, and to put on the new self, created after the likeness of God in true righteousness and holiness. (Ephesians 4:20–24, emphasis added)

Each day, we're invited to undergo this three-part process, like getting cleaned up physically. Imagine coming into the house after a long day digging in a field. You're covered with dirt and dust, your clothes are filthy, and you feel grimy. What do you do? You first remove your old clothes, then you take a shower, and finally, you put on clean clothes.

Every day, we're bombarded with the "filth" of a sinful world. This may come from media, people, and even our own thoughts and temptations. We badly need cleaning! So we regularly put off our old selves by confessing our sins and ensuring that we follow Jesus. Paul says in Colossians 3:5–7:

> *Put to death therefore what is earthly in you: sexual immorality, impurity, passion, evil desire, and covetousness, which is idolatry. On account of these the wrath of God is coming. In these you too once walked, when you were living in them.*

We *renew our minds* by focusing on his Word and talking to him about our needs and concerns. As we do, God begins to reveal his will to us for that day. Paul writes in Romans 12:2: "*Do not be conformed to this world, but be transformed by the renewal of your mind, that by testing you may discern what is the will of God, what is good and acceptable and perfect.*"

And finally, we *put on the new self* by choosing to act in ways that please him. In Colossians 3:12–14, Paul continues:

> *Put on then, as God's chosen ones, holy and beloved, compassionate hearts, kindness, humility, meekness, and patience, bearing with one another and, if one has a complaint against another, forgiving each other; as the Lord has forgiven you, so you also must forgive. And above all these put on love, which binds everything together in perfect harmony.*

When we clean up this way each day, we stay on the path and become effective followers of Jesus.

CLEANING UP

The difficulty with this is that many people want to feel better about themselves but try to *act* better without a deep cleaning inside. That's like coming home from the field and putting on a new suit or dress over your work clothes. You may look better, but underneath, you're still a mess.

This is what the religious leaders did in Jesus' day, and he wasn't too impressed, to say the least!

> *Woe to you, scribes and Pharisees, hypocrites! For you are like whitewashed tombs, which outwardly appear beautiful, but within are full of dead people's bones and all uncleanness. So you also outwardly appear righteous to others, but within you are full of hypocrisy and lawlessness.* (Matthew 23:27–28)

Think about a tomb or a grave with a decomposing body inside. Disgusting! No matter how nicely you dress it up, it doesn't change how dead and repulsive it is inside. Similarly, until we're made inwardly clean by God, no amount of "window dressing" will matter.

In John 13, when Jesus was washing the disciples' feet, Peter—who else?—initially resisted:

> *He came to Simon Peter, who said to him, "Lord, do you wash my feet?" Jesus answered him, "What I am doing you do not understand now, but afterward you will understand." Peter said to him, "You shall never wash my feet." Jesus answered him, "If I do not wash you, you have no share with me."* (John 13:6–8)

Peter didn't understand that Jesus was giving them an example of servanthood and an object lesson of how people all need to be cleansed by him to be his followers. Of course, then Peter wanted a bath!

> *Simon Peter said to him, "Lord, not my feet only but also my hands and my head!" Jesus said to him, "The one who has bathed does not need to wash, except for his feet, but is completely clean. And you are clean, but not every one of*

you." For he knew who was to betray him; that was why
he said, "Not all of you are clean." (John 13:9–11)

Peter had put his faith in Jesus, so he was clean—forgiven and righteous in God's eyes. But Jesus also knew that one of them, Judas, would betray him and never repent. Jesus could wash him with water, but Judas needed true renewal and cleansing through faith in Jesus.

BAPTISM

One of the first things new believers did in the early church days was to get physically baptized. This baptism did not *save* them, but it was an object lesson to show they *had* been saved. It also served to proclaim to everyone their choice to identify with Jesus.

Spiritually, when they first believed, they died to sin, were cleansed by God, and were raised to new life in Jesus. Physically, they showed this by going under the water (dying), being in the water (getting cleansed), and coming up from under the water (being resurrected to new life). This is similar to putting off, renewing, and putting on. Having died to sin, we are called to walk a new path—in the newness of life.

> *What shall we say then? Are we to continue in sin that grace may abound? By no means! How can we who died to sin still live in it? Do you not know that all of us who have been baptized into Christ Jesus were baptized into his death? We were buried therefore with him by baptism into death, in order that, just as Christ was raised from the dead by the glory of the Father, we too might walk in newness of life ... So you also must consider yourselves dead to sin and alive to God in Christ Jesus.* (Romans 6:1–4, 11)

One of the first actions to take as a believer is to get baptized, demonstrating your faith and new life in Jesus. This helps put us on the right path and keeps us accountable for what we have said we believe.

STOP ATTENDING CHURCH

Conventional wisdom says attending church will also help keep you on the right path, but this is not necessarily so. In fact, I would suggest that we all need to stop *attending* church.

Church attendance has declined over the last few years, especially among the college demographic. When they move out on their own, many find that church isn't the priority it was for their parents. Lots of people have reasons why they avoid church. Do you identify with any of these?

- "Sunday is my only day to sleep in."
- "I don't connect with the music."
- "The church is filled with hypocrites."
- "Worship is a private thing for me."
- "I hate being asked to give money."
- "I don't like standing around making small talk."

I had no choice but to go to church as a child. My dad would be in the car early every Sunday morning, warming it up and urging us to hurry. In his opinion, we were late if we were not ten to fifteen minutes early. It's like how the car's gas tank was "empty" if it got below halfway.

> BONUS TIP: These sorts of things happen when you become a parent. Learn to embrace it.

After a twenty-minute drive, during which we rarely felt like talking, we finally got to church. First there was Sunday school. It was aimed at kids and somewhat bearable, but I had a tough time sitting still. Apparently they had a hard time keeping me in my chair instead of under the table. I eventually (mostly) grew out of that, but I still just wanted to run around and play after a week of school.

The church service felt painful and tedious. To start, we sang the "Doxology"—a cappella—and it went downhill from there. In my opinion, the hymns were dry, and the sermons even more so. At least when I was little they had "junior church," which got us out of the sermon, but I still often went home with a big headache.

Sure, I see the value in it now. After all, I was taught—and I believed at a young age—that Jesus loved me and died on the cross for me. So I knew that church was important. It helped form me, providing the building blocks of biblical education. I memorized many Bible verses, some of which I still remember, and I knew what it meant to follow Jesus. It just wasn't all that *enjoyable*, and I can see why many people stop attending when they get old enough to choose.

The problem with attending church is this: we just *attend* church. We're passive consumers, soaking it in, and it's easy to get bored or feel critical of what's produced for us. And if a church disappoints us, we can always go somewhere else. Many people end up church-hopping until they find one they think meets their needs. Until it doesn't.

What is the primary purpose of the church? To meet our needs? Or are we looking at it all wrong? The Church, according to the Bible, isn't a building. It's the followers of Jesus *wherever* they gather to worship God, learn together, serve one another, and reach out to their community. That's why we need to stop *attending* church and start *being* the church.

We will often be disappointed if we just show up and expect our needs to be met. Why do we expect an hour-long service to fix what we've done the rest of the week? That's not what the Church is all about. Everything changes when we shift our attitude from *attending* a church to *participating* as a vital member of Christ's body. When we start serving, using our gifts, caring for others, and reaching out to the community, it soon stops being all about me.

WHAT THE CHURCH IS REALLY ALL ABOUT

I didn't understand this until my high school years—when I became involved with our church youth group and began *serving* instead of just showing up. I also started serving in the bigger church as I could, such as being an usher or even helping out in the nursery as needed.

I first met my wife, Leanne, when I went to her young adults group searching for volunteers to help mentor some troubled youth I was working with—and she volunteered! Though she wasn't keen on working with youth, she was keen on serving Jesus however she could. I later learned that she did many things behind the scenes to help out, such as the menial task of refilling the church pews with offering envelopes, pencils, and prayer cards—in an eight-hundred-seat auditorium. She was also involved in helping run the young adults group. She was willing to serve wherever there was a need. She didn't just "attend church."

In Ephesians 4:11–13, talking about Jesus and his church, the Apostle Paul wrote these words:

> And [Jesus] gave the apostles, the prophets, the evangelists, the shepherds and teachers, to equip the saints for the work of ministry, for building up the body of Christ, until we all attain to the unity of the faith and of the knowledge of the Son of God, to mature manhood, to the measure of the stature of the fullness of Christ …

Note that Jesus gave us shepherds—pastors—and teachers "*to equip the saints.*" Why? So Christians could show up every Sunday and enjoy music and a sermon? No! It says that they are to *equip* the saints—the Church—*for the works of ministry*.

As we serve (doing the "*works of ministry*"), we become unified, mature, and Christ-like, empowered to live and serve even better. My pastor's role is to equip *me* to serve, become Christ-like, and reach out to my community. He's not there to ensure that I enjoy his sermon or the music. As a shepherd, he points me to healthy food, but I shouldn't expect him to hand-feed me.

I have no idea how we ever got this idea that the Christian life is about attending church once a week and then living our lives however we want. Who could read the New Testament, see the people of God turning the world upside down by the power of the Spirit, and then decide that "going to church" is what we're called to do? That would be ridiculous if it wasn't so sad.

It's been suggested that the Church exists to "comfort the afflicted and to afflict the comfortable." This is so true! Please, Lord, when I'm too comfortable, send me people to shake me and wake me up. But when I'm hurting, send those who can help me through those difficult times. All too often the church gets this entirely backward. The ones needing awakening are coddled (especially if they're rich or influential), while those needing help are turned away (especially if they're poor or "different"). Before we jump on the hypocrisy of that, let's look inwardly and remind ourselves that *we* are the Church. If we're not part of the solution, we're part of the problem.

If we go to church and expect to be entertained or taught something simply to add to our knowledge but aren't willing to take action with what we learn … well, no wonder we're bored with "church"! That's not being the Church! That's going to a show, and we've missed the point.

The Church is not a *building*, nor is it a *service* with singing and a speaker. It's a *group of believers* gathering in *community* to worship, learn, grow, serve, and then take what they've experienced to the world. If we allow ourselves or our families to just *go to church*, we have missed what it's all about. And we'll probably end up hating it and searching for a better church.

SPIRITUAL HEALTH

We should be like a source of fresh water that is constantly renewed and refreshes those around us. For a lake to be clean and healthy, it needs fresh water sources flowing in *and* fresh water sources flowing out of it.

If a lake lacks freshwater intakes, it will eventually dry up completely. However, if it's missing the outlets, it will stagnate, like the Dead Sea: salty and smelly. Some Christians are like the Dead Sea—they go to church, hear sermons, sing choruses, read their Bibles, and attend Bible studies, but then they do *nothing* with all that knowledge and information. They have nice, clean intakes, but it stagnates within them because it just sits there.

There are also Christians who dry up because they try to do it all independently. They don't bother to gather with believers, but they're off "doing good" and serving wherever they go. Over time, this becomes unsustainable, and they dry up because they don't have the community of Christ. They are missing the intakes so necessary for their health. Those people often become bitter that no one is helping them, yet they avoid or reject the body of believers they need.

Healthy Christians continually give and receive. They're part of a weekly gathering to be built up and fueled for future service and ministry opportunities. They serve in the church and in their communities. When they return to the gathering, they look forward to being filled up again so they can empty themselves throughout the week. A healthy rhythm in life includes regular involvement with a local church—not for entertainment, but for healthy giving and receiving.

> **BONUS TIP:** Finding a new church is sometimes helpful, but understand that *different* isn't always the same as *better*. It's easy to blame the church when we're not growing, but often it is *we* who need to change, not the church.

God has given us all spiritual gifts for mutual edification within the church, and he has intentionally made the church such that we need one another. When my brother or sister in Christ refuses to come and be part of our church, I miss out. My choice not to get involved or serve harms all of us, not just me. I need the church, and the church needs me. Again, don't simply *attend* church. *Be* the church.

SPIRITUAL DISCIPLINES

To remain on the path, you need to practice staying healthy.

Unhealthy practices lead to wandering in directions that take us far from Christ, but God's Word and history show us the way forward. While we maintain health corporately by serving in the church, our private disciplines also help keep us on track.

We've already touched on some of the disciplines that serve us well:

- Bible study—reading, meditation, memorization
- Prayer—God's priorities and our needs
- Giving generously

- Serving with our gifts
- Confessing our sins
- Living simply as good stewards

Jesus also talks of **fasting**, which means to go without food for a time to focus on prayer. It can be as simple as missing a meal to pray during that time or as severe as going a day or several days with only water to keep you going. I have seasons when I fast more or less, but at the very least, when there's a big prayer concern, I will miss a meal and pray instead. In our culture, fasting from social media, phones, video games, or anything else that holds us captive can also be very helpful.

The benefits of fasting are many. It reminds us of our utter dependence on God. It clears our minds for prayer and helps us focus on the even more important need at hand. It allows us extra time in the day to spend with God, and it even helps us remember and identify with those who regularly don't have enough to eat. Try just missing lunch sometime and going to a quiet place to pray instead. After the initial discomfort, you'll be glad you did!

Another necessary spiritual discipline is **rest**. God set a precedent for us in creation by resting from his work on the seventh day. This was long before the Jews had their Sabbath laws, and the break from work wasn't for God's benefit but ours! Rest helps us stay on the path and energizes us for what lies ahead. It's another essential spiritual rhythm in our lives, where we work hard and then rest well. Sometimes going to bed early is the most spiritual thing we can do.

Something else that many may not recognize as a spiritual discipline is the concept of **celebration**. The Jews had many "feasts," which were times to come together to celebrate the goodness of God. Christians should be the most joyful people in the world, even amid trials. There are times to mourn and times to laugh and celebrate—both are parts of a healthy rhythm.

Finally, **silence and solitude** can be excellent for the soul! Sometimes it's precious to simply be alone and silent before God. We live in a world where people often seem to require music or background noise to be ubiquitous, but maybe we need to turn off the noise and get away from the distractions to truly hear God's voice. I've often spent time alone in God's creation, quietly praying and then waiting upon him.

> **BONUS TIP:** I have found that taking prayer walks in the woods or somewhere quiet has been very helpful. But what I didn't expect was the amazing power of praying out loud when by myself in a car or at home. Although awkward at first, it makes my prayers feel so much more real. Give it a try!

WORSHIP

A lifestyle or rhythm of worship deserves its own chapter, but that will have to be for a different book.

I heard about someone who came out of a church service and said, "I didn't enjoy the worship today." Their friend replied, "That's okay. It wasn't for *you*, anyway!" Although we benefit from worshiping well, it is *for* God. It's never about doing something to make me feel good (though good feelings may accompany it); it is proclaiming God's worth to the world, making much about him.

Have you ever sung in a church service and simply not "felt it"? That happens to me often. I need to continually remind myself that worship is not what I *feel* but what I *give*. Worship is so much more than singing. Oswald Chambers suggests, "Worship is giving God the best that he has given you."[6]

In the Old Testament, we see this in the sacrificial system. The people of God were to bring the *first fruits* of their harvests, the best of their animals, to sacrifice to God. In the New Testament, *we* are the sacrifice, according to Romans 12:1: "*I appeal to you therefore, brothers, by the mercies of God, to present your bodies as a living sacrifice, holy and acceptable to God, which is your spiritual worship.*" True worship, therefore, may include financial giving, helping others, or using our gifts to serve God. No matter what we're doing, if we do it for God, and our hearts are in the right place, it is true worship.

I love the story of Eric Liddell, a Scottish athlete who was also training to be a missionary in China. The award-winning movie *Chariots of Fire* was made about him. There's a great scene in the movie—and true to his life—where he explains to his sister that the missionary work must wait because he believes he needs to honor God by running in the 1924 Olympics. He says, "God made me for a purpose. God made me fast, and when I run, I feel his pleasure."[7] God made each one of us with unique gifts and abilities. When we use them for his glory, it's worship! If God gave you talent as an artist, worship him with that talent. If you're a plumber, always do your best with your abilities. Give back the best he has given you as a living sacrifice to God, holy and acceptable to him.

Eric Liddell worshiped God by running fast, by doing what God had made him good at. But when the 1924 Olympics came, the one-hundred-meter race, which he was highly favored to win, was scheduled on a Sunday. He didn't believe he could honor God by running on the day he'd set aside for rest and time with God, so he forfeited his spot in the race. Winning a gold medal meant much less to him than honoring God.

He was still able to compete in his weaker race, the four-hundred-meters, and somehow, he won the gold medal! He honored God, and then God honored him. Yet at the peak of his athletic career and fame, he quit sports forever to serve God in China, where no one knew him or cared how fast he was. Why? Because that's what God called him to do. He responded in obedience and worship, using his teaching gifts to bring many people to Jesus. During World War Two, Eric became a prisoner in a Japanese internment camp, where he died in 1945, not long before the war ended. But he kept his faith and is now worshiping Jesus with the angels in heaven.

Worship entails more than attending church one day a week and praising Jesus in song. It's giving back to God the very best he has given us in all parts of our lives. We need to be living sacrifices.

WALKING THE GOOD WAY

"Thus says the Lord: 'Stand by the roads, and look, and ask for the ancient paths, where the good way is; and walk in it, and find rest for your souls'" (Jeremiah 6:16a).

It's easy to get off the path, so we need to wisely choose how we fill our minds and act out what we know to be true. By focusing on Jesus in our private lives and in community (the Church), we can follow the path God has set for us. If we do, we'll find ourselves satisfied in him, and he will bring rest to our souls.

CHOOSE YOUR OWN ADVENTURE

The Wise Path: I choose to keep my eyes on Jesus, serving and worshiping him in all aspects of my life.

The Foolish Path: I choose to live for myself and ignore my need for constant renewal.

— Chapter Eight —

HELPING OTHERS FIND THE WAY

And he said to them, "Go into all the world
and proclaim the gospel to the whole creation.
Whoever believes and is baptized will be saved,
but whoever does not believe will be condemned."
~ Mark 16:15–16

It was a beautiful day for a hike, but with everyone else busy, I decided to head out on my own. I grabbed my day pack holding my water bottle, snacks, waterproof shell jacket, compass (in case my phone with GPS died), multi-tool knife, and a small emergency kit. I was ready to go!

> **BONUS TIP:** As the Scouts say, "Be prepared!" That goes for life in general, not just the outdoors.

I drove about an hour to the trailhead, but the time passed quickly with the sun shining and my radio blaring. Soon I was out on the trail, which started with a steady climb. Half an hour in, I took a quick break for a few sips of water, checked my phone app to ensure I was still heading the right way, and continued up the trail. After another half hour or so, I reached my first destination—a small, isolated lake. I was sitting on a log beside the lake when I first smelled the smoke.

My first thought was, *Ah, campfires.* I always love hiking near campgrounds where food is cooking and you can enjoy the smell of everyone's campfire. However, my second thought immediately followed: *Wait, there are no campgrounds for miles. There shouldn't be smoke!* My third, fourth, and fifth thoughts followed quickly: *I need to figure out where that's coming from, I really hope that's not a forest fire I'm smelling,* and *I really need to get away from that!*

I grabbed some grass and tossed it in the air to determine which way the wind was blowing. Chances were, if I could smell the fire but not see or hear it, I was downwind from it. I quickly ascertained that the wind was blowing from the direction I had set out, which was terrible news. That meant it wouldn't do to head back to my car. I returned to the trail and threw more grass in the air. Again the breeze was coming from my starting point. Worst of all, I was downwind from a potential fire and uphill from it. Forest fires can climb hillsides very quickly. Hopefully it wasn't big and would be easily contained.

Glancing at the map on my phone app, I could see a viewpoint not far ahead on the trail, so I decided to hike up further to see what I could from there. Being in the thick trees decreased my visibility, but hopefully the lookout would be more revealing. As I began to walk with urgency, I heard some voices. Soon two young men and two young women appeared on the trail, coming towards me.

"Hey, folks," I began, "do you smell that smoke? I think it's coming from below us. I'm heading up further to see if I can see what's going on. You might not want to head that way right now!"

Both girls looked concerned, and one of the guys did too. But the other one, a hefty man with a thick beard, said, "Okay, thanks. We'll be careful." He continued on his way.

"Seriously," I said, "don't go that way until we know the situation. There's a viewpoint up ahead, and I'm hoping it will tell me where the fire is."

The fellow stopped, looked me in the eye, and said, "Yeah, thanks. We were just up there, and we didn't see anything. It's probably just a campfire." He proceeded to walk down the trail, and the others stopped, looked at me, looked at him, and then followed him down. I could hear some worried discussion as soon as they walked, but they continued towards the fire.

A few minutes later, I reached the viewpoint, and sure enough, I could see thick smoke wafting from below. Hoping to alert the group I had met, I began to yell, "Fire! There's a fire down below!" I don't know if they heard me, but at this point, I knew I needed to get up the hill quickly and away from it. I began to walk rapidly up the hill. Ten minutes later, I heard a helicopter, which I figured was good news. That meant someone in authority knew about the fire. Hopefully they would send water bombers to put it out. I couldn't count on that, so I kept moving quickly.

The slight breeze I had felt behind me earlier was picking up strength, and I worried that the fire was getting closer. I stopped to look at my phone app again and saw that the canyon I had earlier set out to reach wasn't far. That was when genuine fear began to set in. A canyon! The map showed no way across it, so if that fire was coming up behind me, I could be stuck between the two.

Just then, I saw an older couple walking towards me. This time I simply shouted, "Fire! There's a forest fire down there! Don't go that way!"

At almost that exact moment, I heard a movement behind me, and the foursome I had met earlier were running up the hill, out of breath. "Fire!" one of them gasped. By now we couldn't only smell the smoke but we also saw it as it billowed up the hill.

"Let's move!" I exclaimed, and all seven of us hurried up the path. I wanted to run ahead of them, but I felt it was my responsibility to see them all to safety. I stayed just ahead, urging them forward. But our progress was much too slow for my liking.

A few minutes later, we reached the canyon, and I quickly scanned the area for a way down into it. But all I saw were steep cliffs, probably at least a hundred feet to the bottom. I saw a rock jutting out, a wire fence to keep people safe, and many signs warning people to stay away from the edge.

The older woman among us was gasping for breath, and in a panicked voice she asked, "What do we do?"

The older man, who I assume was her husband, answered, "It'll be okay. The fire probably won't get this far." However, based on the smoke that now enveloped us, we all knew it was coming.

Again I grabbed my phone to see if my map showed any other ways out of there, but I could see none. I had also brought a topographical map I'd printed off—just in case—but again, it looked like the trail ended right there. A bit to the west was a faint line across the canyon. Could that be a bridge? I told the others of my faint hope, and we could see a narrow path along the canyon wall heading in that direction.

As I began to lead the group that way, the older man chose that moment to argue with me. "There's nothing there! I guarantee it! I've been in these parts all my life, and I've *never* seen any way across this canyon. We'd have to go at least three miles to the east to get around it."

His wife objected immediately. "But Sam, what about that cable car? Your brother mentioned that once, remember?"

"Bill was a *fool*, Margaret. Always acting as if he knew so much! He knew *nothing!*"

I figured any chance was worth a try, so I said, "Staying here is a death sentence! Please come. It's not safe here."

The four young people agreed and trotted towards the trail, but the older man dug in and refused to go. Seeing his refusal, his wife decided to stay with him. I could see the fear in her eyes, so I tried one last time to urge them to join us.

"You all go ahead," the old man said. "Help is on its way, and I want us to be where they can find us."

I wanted to argue, but I knew that time was running out, so I prayed silently for their safety and followed the others along the small path to the west. It soon all but disappeared, and we were fighting through branches and brambles. We could hear helicopters and smell the smoke, but there were no flames so far. I wondered if we should have stayed put and hoped for rescue like the older couple. Yet given the smoke, I doubted anyone could see them on the lookout.

After about ten minutes of pushing through the bushes, we came out at the canyon again, and I asked the others if they could see anything with their younger eyes. They shook their heads, but then one of them said, "Yes, I think I see something! It might be a cable?"

We forced our way further, and soon we saw she was right. There was a cable right across the chasm. We walked around a large boulder a few minutes later and found where the line was attached. To my delight and relief, a cable car was sitting on our side of the canyon!

However, the bearded fellow would have none of it. "Are you kidding me? That thing will never hold us! The cable will snap! Look how old it is! There's no way I'm getting in!"

"Listen," I said sternly, "we have little choice. This canyon goes for miles, and the fire will be here before we can possibly get around it. We have this one chance, and we need to take it! It looks solid to me, and there's room in the car for all of us. Gravity will take us a little past the middle, and then we'll pull ourselves up the rest of the way. It'll be fine."

"You guys go ahead. If it works, send it back, and I might try it," the bearded fellow said.

The girl, who I assume was his wife or girlfriend, agreed. "No way I'm getting in that thing."

Suddenly we heard the crackling of flames not far away. "You guys!" I exclaimed. "The fire's right behind us! This is our only chance!"

The smaller guy looked at his friends, then towards the fire, and quickly climbed into the basket. The girl with him climbed in, and I followed suit. "Get in, you guys!" I urged the other couple.

But the bearded man ignored me, grabbed his girl by the hand, and quickly headed farther west. I could hear him telling her, "Let's keep going. There must be a better way across."

I quickly untied the basket, gave a little shove, and we began to gain speed along the cable. Minutes later, we were safe on the other side. We never saw any of the others again.

THE FIRE IS COMING

Although the above story is fictional (sorry!), I believe it's a truthful metaphor for our spiritual lives.

> **BONUS TIP:** If you tell a story as if it really happened, be sure to make it clear at some point that you made it up! Some people are very loose with the truth in their stories ...

Consider: we are all on a trail. At some point, we must decide what to do about eternity. The fire behind us and the chasm before us represent the certainty of our coming deaths. The time will come; we just don't know when. According to the Word of God, there is only one way to live forever: by putting our faith in Jesus Christ—the cable car in this analogy. There's room for everyone, but you have to choose to get in.

Before Jesus began his earthly ministry, God sent John the Baptizer to prepare people for Jesus' salvation message. Multitudes came to hear him preach, and many chose to show their repentance by having him baptize them. Yet read what John proclaimed to those who came with insincere motives:

> *You brood of vipers! Who warned you to flee from the wrath to come? Bear fruits in keeping with repentance. And do not begin to say to yourselves, "We have Abraham as our father." For I tell you, God is able from these stones to raise up children for Abraham. Even now the axe is laid to the root of the trees. Every tree therefore that does not bear good fruit is cut down and thrown into the fire.* (Luke 3:7b–9)

John knew that God's wrath was coming. He warned these Jews that just because they came from the line of Abraham and were thus "God's chosen people" didn't mean they were safe. Yes, repent and be baptized, but understand that physical baptism can't save you. True repentance results in right living.

The crowds asked him what they should do. Somehow, they knew baptism was not enough, and John gave them examples of the life that trusts in God. Interestingly, all three examples he provided have to do with how people's hearts respond to money (Luke 3:12–14):

- *"Collect no more than you are authorized to do."*
- *"Do not extort money from anyone ..."*
- *"... be content with your wages."*

John knew that their hearts would be with their treasures. Next, John introduced them to Jesus and gave another warning of God's judgment—the coming fire:

> *I baptize you with water, but he who is mightier than I is coming, the strap of whose sandals I am not worthy to untie. He will baptize you with the Holy Spirit and fire. His winnowing fork is in his hand, to clear his threshing floor and to gather the wheat into his barn, but the chaff he will burn with unquenchable fire.* (Luke 3:16b–17)

"But," you may say, "that was 'Crazy John'! He ate locusts and dressed weirdly!" True. Yet John's message only foreshadowed Jesus, who spoke more about the coming judgment than anyone else in the Bible. Take Matthew 13:47–50, for example, where Jesus taught this parable:

> *Again, the kingdom of heaven is like a net that was thrown into the sea and gathered fish of every kind. When it was full, men drew it ashore and sat down and sorted the good into containers but threw away the bad. So it will be at the end of the age. The angels will come out and separate the evil from the righteous and throw them into the fiery furnace. In that place there will be weeping and gnashing of teeth.*

Jesus continuously warned the people of coming judgment, that they needed to get right with God and put their trust in him only. Otherwise, they would be thrown into the fire. This phrase, *"weeping and gnashing of teeth,"* demonstrating utter misery, is used by Jesus many times to warn people away from the path of evil. In Matthew 25:41b, he says to those who didn't trust in God and live for him: *"Depart from me, you cursed, into the eternal fire prepared for the devil and his angels."*

CALLED TO WARN OTHERS

Judgment is a challenging topic, and some Christians have chosen the unbiblical path of denying hell's existence. To reconcile what they believe God is like, they ignore the plain words of the Old Testament prophets, John, Jesus, his disciples, and so on. This is understandable, as it's a difficult doctrine to comprehend or accept. It often comes from our inability to truly grasp God's holiness. We tend to emphasize his love instead (see chapter two).

> **BONUS TIP:** There's a popular and unbiblical movement today to deny the existence of hell. Don't get caught up in it unless you want to ignore a significant portion of Jesus' teaching. Ignoring or denying hell won't make it go away.

If we deny the clear teaching of the scriptures on hell, we'll also fail in God's calling to warn others away from it. In Ezekiel 33, God speaks of watchmen who guard the city against enemies. He says that if the watchman sees the enemy coming, he *must* blow his trumpet and warn the people. If the people ignore the warning, their blood is on their own hands. In other words, they have no one to blame but themselves. However, if the watchman sees the enemy and *fails* to blow the trumpet, he is to blame for everyone who dies.

Similarly, in the New Testament, those who follow Jesus are called to be heralds of the gospel. This is what it literally means in Mark 16:15 when Jesus told his disciples, "*Go into all the world and proclaim the gospel to the whole creation.*" *Proclaim* here means speaking out, or *shouting*, as a herald. What did heralds do? They stood on street corners under their king's authority and declared what the people needed to hear.

We are watchmen; we are heralds, and we are also witnesses. Jesus' last words to his disciples before he ascended into heaven were, "*But you will receive power when the Holy Spirit has come upon you, and you will be my witnesses in Jerusalem and in all Judea and Samaria, and to the end of the earth*" (Acts 1:8). Jesus knew the believers would soon be scattered by persecution. As they traveled, wherever they went, they were to tell others about what they had seen and experienced with Jesus.

What do watchmen, heralds, and witnesses have in common? They are all trusted to proclaim what they know to be true and not shy away from it. They don't dare disobey and keep it to themselves. When there is good news, they share it. When there is bad news, they warn the people.

GOOD NEWS AND BAD NEWS

In a nutshell, the gospel is the good news that people can be forgiven for their sins and reconciled to God through the death and resurrection of Jesus, his Son. This means true freedom and eternal life.

The challenging part of sharing the gospel is that most people don't know or understand their *need* for salvation. If you walked up to someone on the street and told them they could be saved by putting their faith in Jesus, many would reply, "Saved from what?" To understand how great the good news is, people must have some idea of how terrible the bad news is. They must comprehend that their sins have put them directly in line with the wrath of a holy God.

We love to quote John 3:16: "*For God so loved the world, that he gave his only Son, that whoever believes in him should not perish but have eternal life.*" Yet we often fail to put this verse in proper context. The contrast to the good news in verse 16 comes in verse 18: "*Whoever believes in him is not condemned, but whoever does not believe is condemned already, because he has not believed in the name of the only Son of God.*" We see a similar contrast in John 3:36: "*Whoever believes in the Son has eternal life; whoever does not obey the Son shall not see life, but the wrath of God remains on him.*"

I can't think of anything worse than God's wrath. The very thought of it directed at me would paralyze me with fear. That's what makes it so amazing that I can enjoy a right relationship with God through Jesus. The terrible news of God's wrath gives context to the fantastic news of God's forgiveness. Good news is only understood as good in light of bad news.

For example, it can be very uncomfortable to have a wart. I've had one on the ball of my foot, and it hurt every step I took. My doctor burned it off several times over many months, but it kept growing back.

If someone produced a pill I could swallow, and the wart would go away, I'd say that would be pretty good news! To someone who has never had a wart, it maybe wouldn't impress them so much, but for one who has experienced the bad news of a painful wart, it would be wonderful.

Yet as nasty as warts can be, they aren't nearly as bad as having cancer. When my best friend, Dan, fought cancer, it was horrible to watch him deteriorate. I am still grieved when I remember watching him perish in less than a year from such a terrible disease. Had there been a pill to swallow that could have healed him of cancer, he would have gladly taken it! There would have been *much* rejoicing! And we would tell everyone else we knew who was dying from cancer, "*Believe me!*" Why? Because a proven cure for cancer would be incredibly good news, and good news must be shared!

Clearly, a cure for cancer would be so much better news than a cure for warts. Why? Because the bad news of cancer is so much worse than the bad news of warts. You can live with a wart, but cancer kills. So the good news of the cure is proportionate to the bad news of the disease. Imagine offering the cure to someone who doesn't know they have cancer or won't admit they have it. You, or maybe a doctor, would first have to convince them of the bad news of their cancer before the good news of the cure would mean anything to them.

This is one of the problems we have with sharing the gospel message. People don't believe in a holy God, they don't believe in his wrath, and they have no clue that they're dying in their sins on a path that leads to destruction. They deny that fire is coming. For someone to understand the incredibly good news of what Jesus did for them on the cross, they must first understand the terrible news of their sin disease. We do a disfavor to people when we ignore the issue of sin and tell them they just need to accept Jesus into their hearts or add him as a friend.

Without repentance, there is no salvation. You can't repent if you don't know you're a sinner, and you can't know you're a sinner if you don't believe in a holy God.

BONUS TIP: Never present Jesus as an "add-on" to people's lives to make them feel better, like dessert after supper. "Enjoy your meal—your life—but save a little room for Jesus at the end."

THE CHASM

In the analogy of a forest fire, consider a few things. First, the *fire* represents the unrelenting march of time in everyone's life until the day their death comes. Every one of us will reach the chasm one day—it is inescapable. We don't know when we'll die, but the day is coming. Most of us will probably live into our seventies and eighties, or even a little longer, but there are no guarantees that we won't die today. As Hebrews 9:27 states, "... *it is appointed for man to die once, and after that comes judgment* ..."

Second, the *warnings* are there. As discussed in chapter two, God is knowable and has revealed himself in creation, so we are all without excuses. We can ignore the warnings and run towards the fire or just wait for it to overtake us, but none of us can say God was unfair.

Third, our *ability* isn't what matters. If the seven hikers had lined up at the chasm and tried to jump to escape the fire, it wouldn't matter that the younger people could jump farther than the older people. Even if they were the best long jumpers in the world, they wouldn't have made it. They would have *no advantage* over someone old or in a wheelchair. When we compare ourselves to those around us, we make one of two mistakes: either we despair because we can never be as good as someone else, or we are elated that we are better than others. But God doesn't grade on a curve. As Romans 3:23 tells us, "*all have sinned.*" We are equal at the foot of the cross. No one can make it on their own strength or goodness.

Fourth, it's only by *faith* that we are saved. Putting our faith in Jesus means we look at the chasm of sin that separates us from God, then we look at Jesus, and we believe that he's our only hope of getting across. As Ephesians 2:8–9 declares, "*For by grace you have been saved through faith. And this is not your own doing; it is the gift of God, not a result of works, so that no one may boast.*"

Faith in Jesus is the only way to God. First Timothy 2:5–6a says, "*For there is one God, and there is one mediator between God and men, the man Christ Jesus, who gave himself as a ransom for all* ..."

THE BRIDGE

One of the tools I've often used to explain how the good news solves our separation from God is just a single verse, Romans 6:23, and a sketch: *"For the wages of sin is death, but the gift of God is eternal life in Christ Jesus our Lord."*

Using a napkin or scrap piece of paper, I draw a person on one side of a chasm and God on the other, with the chasm marked "sin & death." On the left, under the person, I write the bad news: "the wages of sin is death."

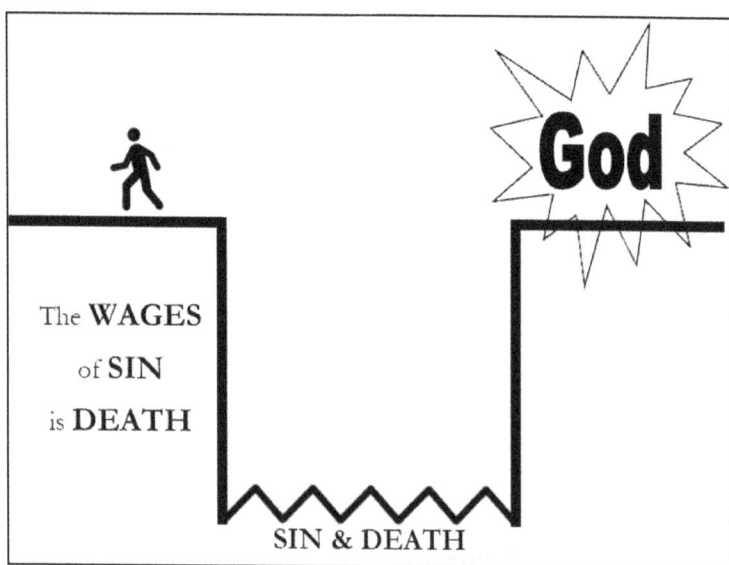

The **WAGES**
of **SIN**
is **DEATH**

God

SIN & DEATH

I explain that sin is simply disobeying the moral law God has written on our hearts and in his Word. It's doing what we know we *should not* do and not doing what we know we *should* do. Wages are what we earn, what we deserve, so *death* is the wage we earn for rebelling against God.

But there is good news! I write on the other side of the chasm, under God, "But the gift of God is eternal life." A gift is something received freely, not earned. God wants us to live in a proper relationship with him forever, but we can do nothing to gain that. Therefore, he provides it freely as a gift. The bad news is that we earn death from sin, but the good news is that we can receive eternal life from God as a free gift.

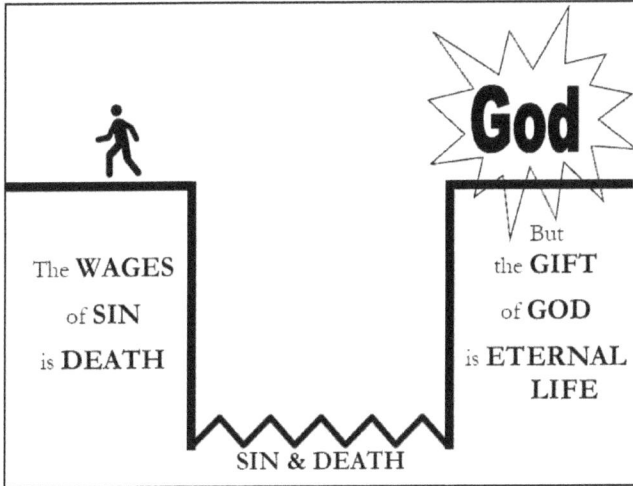

The question then remains: *how?* How can we receive that gift? I draw a cross over the chasm and label it "through Jesus Christ our Lord." The way to receive God's free gift is "through Jesus Christ"—by acknowledging him as "our Lord." He is our master, and we must accept his death on the cross in payment for our sins. Like a bridge (or even a cable car), Jesus provides us free access to the Father if we put our trust in him to remove our sins and set us free.

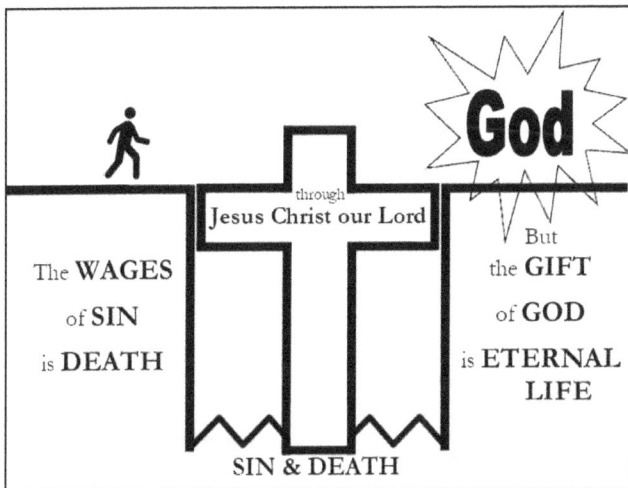

To be forgiven of our sins, receive eternal life, and have a relationship with God, we merely have to cross that bridge by trusting in Jesus.

FOUR FUNDAMENTAL TRUTHS

Many resources explain the gospel in four simple steps we need to understand and believe. I like to explain it with these four fundamental truths of the gospel:

1. God's Plan is LIFE
2. Our Problem is SIN
3. God's Solution is JESUS
4. Our Response is to BELIEVE & RECEIVE

God's plan has always been that we would have true, abundant life in him. But through our sin, we have broken that relationship and placed ourselves under God's righteous judgment. However, God did not abandon us to the results of our sins. He solved our problem by sending Jesus to die on the cross in our place. He was a substitute to pay the penalty for our sins. To be restored to a relationship with God, we need to choose to believe in Jesus and receive his free gift of eternal life.

For verses on these four points and a printable sheet, please see the resources section on my website, cwdouglas.com.

USE WORDS IF NECESSARY?

A few years ago, Leanne and I took some days off and stayed at a hotel in Parksville, British Columbia, a beautiful resort town on Vancouver Island. We ate several meals at the sports bar restaurant in the hotel, and each time we ate there, we continued our practice of praying aloud before our meal. One day, our waitress told us that she had noticed that we prayed before our meals, and we smiled and told her that we are Christians and that we always try to remember to thank God for our food before we eat. She then asked if we'd be willing to pray for one of her co-workers going in for surgery. Of course! We would love to! And so we did, right then and there.

We felt perhaps a little awkward when she then told us the surgery was for breast enhancement, but what mattered was that the surgery was a huge concern for our waitress, and she sincerely wanted prayers for her friend.

> **BONUS TIP:** Simply praying before your meals will make people wonder why you do that, often leading to great conversations. But don't forget to tip well (in countries where that's expected), or you'll only reinforce the stereotype some people have that Christians are cheap. Steward your money carefully, but never cheap-out where you can have a good—or bad—Christian witness.

You may have heard the expression, "Preach the gospel at all times; if necessary, use words." This has often been credited to St. Francis of Assisi, which is historically unfounded and somewhat ironic. St. Francis went from town to town, often *preaching* five or six times per day! I understand why people like the saying. The implication is that our *lives* should preach the gospel so that words will be unnecessary.

Undoubtedly, our lives *should* display the gospel's truth, but the gospel itself is *news*. People can never know what Jesus did for them if no one tells them.

> *How then will they call on him in whom they have not believed? And how are they to believe in him of whom they have never heard? And how are they to hear without someone preaching? And how are they to preach unless they are sent? As it is written, "How beautiful are the feet of those who preach the good news!"* (Romans 10:14–15)

We need to tell people *specifically* about Jesus. At the same time, our lives should be so Christ-like, so full of sacrificial love and kindness, that people want to know about the hope we have within us.

One summer, I worked at a secular camp on Vancouver Island. During staff training, I told people I was a Christian, which evidently got back to the director. He approached me one day to inform me that I wasn't allowed to share my faith with the campers because children are impressionable. I was taken aback by this, especially considering that many of my co-workers drank, smoked, and partied on the weekends. For some reason they were allowed to share their beliefs and lifestyles with the campers, but I wasn't!

However, I submitted to the director's authority and never *started* a conversation about faith with my campers. Of course, I did bring out my Bible and read it where I would be seen by my campers, especially on overnight backpacking trips. Unsurprisingly, these teens often asked, "Hey, what are you reading?" When I told them it was a Bible, they usually asked, "What does it say?" What choice did I have but to answer a sincere question from a camper? Without "sharing my faith," I told kids what the Bible said—the message of the gospel!

I have done the same thing on planes or trains. Simply reading a Bible elicits questions. Praying before meals draws questions. Serving others also causes people to wonder why you do that. Simple acts of kindness show that we are different from the world. And when people ask what we did on the weekend, we can unashamedly tell them we went to church.

THE CHALLENGE

Why do we have such a hard time sharing our faith? Here are three likely reasons. See if you identify with any of these.

1. Association

One of the reasons I'm not quick to identify as a Christian in some circles is that I'm ashamed to be associated with many who claim the name of Christian. In North America today, when people hear that you're a Christian, they will likely associate you with any or all of the following:

- Hatred towards LGBTQ+ individuals
- Hatred towards minority races
- Hatred towards those who've had abortions

- Radical right-wing political views
- Residential school abuses
- American Evangelicalism
- Millionaire "Health & Wealth" preachers

We've had children come to our camp literally afraid of Christians because their parents have spoken regularly about how terrible we are. Hopefully these campers have all gone home knowing that at least some who follow Jesus are wonderful people.

Jesus was also misunderstood and accused of many things he never said or did. Identifying with Jesus means accepting that you *will be* misunderstood, mistreated, and even hated. We need to make sure that if we're hated, it's because of Jesus, not because we're unloving or unkind.

2. Inconsistency

As I grew up, my biggest problem with talking about my faith was that I was afraid to drag down the name of Jesus with my poor attitudes and behaviors. Even today, in the back of my mind, I am very aware that my walk can never match my talk about Jesus.

However, I must remember that I'm not called to be *perfect* in this life. I'm going to fail. Jesus didn't save me because I had it all together. He saved me because I will never have it all together on this side of heaven. Instead of worrying about my inconsistencies, I'm trying to live humbly before God. This means I accept that I'm a work in progress and that God, not I, will bring about the changes in time. When I mess up, I try to be honest and transparent about it. Our message to unbelievers is never, "Look at me—I have it all together," but "Look at Jesus—he can forgive you, just like he's forgiven me."

It's been said that telling others about Jesus is like a beggar telling another beggar where he found bread. I'm still a beggar on this side of heaven, but I know where to find the Bread of Life—Jesus!

3. Unconvinced

Finally, many of us are unconvinced that what we believe is even true. We're not sure that Jesus is truly the "only way." We wonder about the doctrine of hell. We're afraid that the Bible is scientifically or historically inaccurate. We can't explain how a loving God could allow so much evil. We hold on to our faith by tiny threads that are in danger of snapping.

As we discussed in chapter six, doubts are natural. In fact, nothing in this life is 100 percent sure, yet we unthinkingly put our faith in things all day, every day. When I sit in a chair, I believe it will hold my weight. When I eat food from a store, I believe it has been safely made. When I drive through an intersection with a green light, I trust that the light will be red for cars to my left and right.

I don't think about these things, but from my past experiences, I know that it's improbable that they will fail me. Similarly, faith in Jesus isn't based on blindness or ignorance but on the belief that God has been trustworthy in the past and will be dependable in the future. Chairs fail, electronics fail, and even food manufacturing fails, but God always comes through for us. Perhaps that's why the main thing God demands of us is simply *faith*: "*And without faith it is impossible to please him, for whoever would draw near to God must believe that he exists and that he rewards those who seek him*" (Hebrews 11:6).

When God saved the Israelites from Egypt and performed many miracles, some still rebelled and refused to trust in him: "*Therefore, when the Lord heard, he was full of wrath; a fire was kindled against Jacob; his anger rose against Israel, because they did not <u>believe</u> in God and did not <u>trust</u> his saving power*" (Psalm 78:21–22, emphasis added).

God requires us to trust in him, but even that faith doesn't need to be super strong. I love this response from a man who was struggling to believe: "*And Jesus said to him, "'If you can'! All things are possible for one who believes." Immediately the father of the child cried out and said, "I believe; help my unbelief!*" (Mark 9:23–24).

Don't give up if you're unconvinced that Jesus is the only and best way to live. As this father cried out, you can pray for God to help you with your lack of faith—and he will!

You can also talk to mature believers and ask how they deal with their questions and doubts. There are excellent, scholarly answers to our questions. Ask your pastor where to find books and articles that will help you with things you don't understand. The main thing is not to give up. Keep going, keep pressing on, and believe God when he says he is still working in you. Faith is a *journey*, and we don't arrive until we see Jesus face to face. Remember Philippians 1:6: *"And I am sure of this, that he who began a good work in you will bring it to completion at the day of Jesus Christ."*

Don't give up on God—he certainly hasn't given up on you. As you practice your faith, it will become stronger, like a muscle. Then naturally, as you find joy and fulfillment in Jesus, you will share that path with others. As God says in Isaiah 41:10 to all who trust in him: *"Fear not, for I am with you; be not dismayed, for I am your God; I will strengthen you, I will help you, I will uphold you with my righteous right hand."*

CHOOSE YOUR OWN ADVENTURE

The Wise Path: I choose to warn people about the coming fire and lead them to Jesus because the good news is so great, and the bad news is so terrible.

The Foolish Path: I choose to live for myself, convinced that it is safer and more enjoyable than being labeled as a follower of Jesus.

— Chapter Nine —

ADVENTURING WITH PURPOSE

Many are the plans in the mind of a man,
but it is the purpose of the Lord that will stand.
~ Proverbs 19:21

We can wander around for a long time if we don't know where we're going.

After my third year of college on the frozen Canadian prairies, my friend and I borrowed his mother's car and drove down the Oregon coast to do some camping. We were on a tight budget as poor college students, but we figured all we would need to buy was food and gas, so away we went. As for planning, we had a small book with maps and campgrounds and a vague idea of where we wanted to go—south! We were going to wing it, and it would be amazing!

On the first day, we drove from Vancouver down to a campground near Lincoln City, Oregon. The people there were so happy to see us arrive that they threw us a parade. According to the locals, it was a Memorial Day event, but I like to think it was for us.

The following day, we drove to Florence, to a campground surrounded by sand dunes. I remembered being there as a kid with my parents. We set up camp and tried to relax, but it was extremely windy. So at about 1:00 that afternoon, we decided to drive down to San Francisco—just 900 kilometers (550 miles) farther south.

It took almost all night to get there. We slept in the car for a few fitful hours in a rest area just before arriving north of the city. Then we drove around for a long while looking for a campground we'd seen on the map but couldn't find, so we drove over the Golden Gate Bridge into

San Francisco. San Francisco is vast, and we had no idea where to go, so we left! We crossed the Oakland Bridge, drove inland, and finally found a nice campground.

For some reason lost to me now, we decided to start driving north the next day. Perhaps we figured the campgrounds in Oregon were better. After a night at a KOA in Redding, California, we continued north into the mountains of northern California near Ashton. Looking for a campground, we drove up into the hills and finally found it—covered in snow! A few RVs were there for the fishing, but our tent wouldn't cut it. So we drove back down and farther north, but then we hit rain, so we decided to keep going north until we found somewhere not so rainy.

Unfortunately, it didn't stop raining all the way back to Vancouver, so we eventually arrived back at my friend's place. The trip was over, and I wished we'd stayed in California!

> BONUS TIP: Most things that fail do so because of poor planning. Get in the habit of thinking through what you hope to do and writing it out. Plan, then do!

MISSION

It was a fun-ish trip, but it could have been much better. It could have been a fantastic trip had we researched ahead of time and planned things out. Instead, we wasted our time—and gas—driving around without any real sense of where we wanted to go and what we wanted to see. We had no idea what places like San Francisco had to offer, so we drove away, seeing absolutely nothing.

Many people's lives are like that. They have a vague sense that they want certain things out of life such as money, happiness, marriage, and family. So they get some education, try a job for a while, switch to something else, find someone they like, get married for a while, try another job, try another spouse, and eventually settle down with a family, yet they leave behind a trail of broken relationships and wasted opportunities. But if they die with an inheritance to pass on, surrounded by people who care for them, they figure they've lived a good enough life.

That's not enough for me. I want my life to make a difference.

I'm not saying that raising a family well and having loved ones isn't valuable. It certainly is. However, Jesus offers his followers so much more than that. He offers purpose and fulfillment by joining him in building an eternal kingdom.

Most organizations have what they call a "mission statement." This is their purpose for existing. At Timberline Ranch, our mission is "to offer Christian hope and wholeness to young people and families in a safe and fun camping environment." Every word in that statement is intentional. I should know—I was part of the committee that labored long and hard on it.

- *Offer*—presenting a gift that people can receive or reject
- *Christian hope*—the gospel: beginning a relationship with Jesus
- *Christian wholeness*—discipleship: growing in a relationship with Jesus
- *Young people and families*—who the ministry is aimed at
- *Safe and fun*—our programs are first safe and then outrageously fun!
- *Camping environment*—using an outdoor camp setting to accomplish these goals

Whenever we consider adding another program or think about how we will run a camp, this statement is the filter through which everything goes. We don't run seniors' bingo nights, because our mission isn't aimed at seniors. We teach the gospel clearly and often in our programs because that is our mission. But we don't shove it down people's throats because that is not our mission.

My personal mission statement is a work in progress, but here is the current iteration:

For the glory of God, I desire to be a man of integrity and purpose, using all he has given me to help people

experience the joy of knowing Jesus and living for
him.

This means that I refuse to settle for mediocrity in my life. I want to
live for Jesus and make a difference. God has given me so much, and I
want to use it all to help others come to faith in Jesus and grow in that
relationship.

One verse I have chosen as a "life verse" (a verse that has special
meaning to me and helps define my mission in life) is 1 Corinthians
15:58: *"Therefore, my dear brothers and sisters, stand firm. Let nothing
move you. Always give yourselves fully to the work of the Lord, because you
know that your labor in the Lord is not in vain"* (NIV).

My mission in life is based on the premise that giving myself "fully
to the work of the Lord" is worthwhile. So when my path is difficult, I
stand firm on the promises of Jesus that he is with me, is guiding me,
and will one day reward all my efforts. My mission and purpose come
from my relationship with Jesus.

PURPOSE

Does your life have a mission and purpose? What if you could find out
what that is? God has made every one of us with purpose and meaning. He
has given us spiritual gifts, abilities, passions, and experiences that make us
exactly the right person to accomplish what he has planned for us. When
we trusted in him, that purpose began to take shape in our lives. I believe
God has given each of us both a *general* purpose and a *specific* purpose.

Our general purpose as believers is to bring glory to God by doing
good works, or "fruit," as the Bible calls it. Of course, a branch can only
produce fruit by staying connected to the tree or vine. Jesus said:

> *I am the vine; you are the branches. Whoever abides in me
> and I in him, he it is that bears much fruit, for apart from
> me you can do nothing ... By this my Father is glorified,
> that you bear much fruit and so prove to be my disciples.*
> (John 15:5, 8)

Each of us is called to produce fruit by loving God and others, the two greatest commands, according to Jesus (see chapter three). How do we do that? We show our love for God by obeying him (1 John 4:19) and living holy lives dedicated to displaying his greatness (1 Peter 1:16). We demonstrate our love for others by serving them and by "making disciples" wherever we go. Jesus told his followers,

> *Go therefore and make disciples of all nations, baptizing them in the name of the Father and of the Son and of the Holy Spirit, teaching them to observe all that I have commanded you. And behold, I am with you always, to the end of the age.* (Matthew 28:19–20)

We all have the meaningful, general mission of loving God and others and helping people become followers of Jesus and grow in their service to him.

We also each have specific purposes for which God has created us: *"For we are his workmanship, created in Christ Jesus for good works, which God prepared beforehand, that we should walk in them"* (Ephesians 2:10). We are God's workmanship, his masterpiece, created to do amazing things that he planned for us before we were even born! He didn't save us so that we simply would populate heaven one day—he saved us so that we could be involved in accomplishing his great plans. He wants us to walk in those good works and take the trails He charted for us long ago.

I find it amazing that God had specific good works planned for me to bring him glory and make a difference in this world! Understandably then, God also gives us gifts and abilities to carry out those very actions.

God gave me abilities, gifts, and passions to succeed in camp ministry, but I had to discover that over time. I never intended to work at a camp, much less become a camp director. In fact, my first experience as a camper could have turned me off camp forever.

I was eight years old, and a couple of older boys in my cabin picked on me throughout the week. One day they cornered me with no one else around. They had threatened to throw me in the showers with my clothes on. This terrified me, perhaps due to a young boy's natural disinclination to getting too clean. They grabbed me and tried to drag me to the showers, but I wrapped my arms around one of the posts of the cabin, and they had a tough time prying me off it. I was screaming and crying when—thankfully—our cabin leader came by. He told them to let me go, and they reluctantly did so.

It was a rough start to my career at camp, and there were other rough weeks. Once, I got my nose cracked by a kid who intentionally swung a hockey stick at my head. Other times I was injured playing rough games in which we tackled each other and tried to rip armbands off. I got bee stings, skinned knees, sprained ankles, and even whiplash. Yet nothing would stop me from going to camp every summer for nine years, even though I had to earn half of the camp fee myself.

Something kept drawing me back to camp. At sixteen, I took a CIT (Counselor in Training) program and became a cabin leader for several summers. This was incredibly hard at times, and I had weeks at my wits' end trying to deal with difficult boys in my cabin. I also had times of sickness, multiple staph infections, serious injuries, and challenging relationships. After gaining so much experience, I was asked to lead the CIT program for the next two years. I also began a new "Leaders in Training" (LIT) program for the camp.

Perhaps it was natural to work full-time for three years at a camp in Hedley, British Columbia when I graduated from Bible college. Following that, I ran an employment program for troubled teens: "Youth Beyond Bounds." Then I worked for Youth For Christ/Youth Unlimited, running similar programs and working with teenagers in a couple of high schools. After a short time as an associate pastor, followed by graduate studies, I finally became a camp director, which I've been since 2005.

I had no idea I wanted to be a camp director! All I knew was that I wanted to serve God, help young people come to faith in Jesus, and encourage people to grow to be his disciples. God gave me the passion, gifts, and abilities to do those things in a camp setting, yet my focus was on going wherever God led me, not finding the perfect job or position within an organization.

That is the key: surrendering to God and going wherever he leads, not searching for that "perfect job." Some see such surrender as negative, but I disagree. Yes, it means giving up some of our earthly desires, but it also means replacing them with incredible joy and peace. It also deepens our relationship with the God who made us how we are for his purposes.

> **BONUS TIP:** If you're willing to go wherever God leads you, you will become a tremendous tool in his hands, and there is no limit to what he may do through you.

I have learned God's specific purposes for me slowly and often painfully. What has kept me going is the confidence that he created me to do specific good works that he planned for me—and I am the only one who can do them!

JOB, CAREER, OR VOCATION?

Sometimes we put too much emphasis on finding a job or a career when it's a *vocation* we should be pursuing. The difference is this: a *job* is what you do to earn money; a *career* is a job or several similar jobs over a long period, but a *vocation* is your purpose and direction for life. It comes from your beliefs, passions, gifts, abilities, and calling. It comes from *who you are*, not simply *what you do* to earn money.

Sometimes you simply need to get a job. Due to circumstances, many people aren't working in the place of their chosen vocation. They have a family to support or debts to pay off, and they can't afford to wait for the perfect vocation—they just need to survive. The worst thing some people do is put off finding work because they believe they must be in the ideal situation or they're not being "true to themselves." That is a terrible excuse for not working!

> **BONUS TIP:** God ordained work as *good*. Never be ashamed to take a job that helps pay the bills.

Your vocation is not simply about finding the "perfect job"—if such a thing exists. It goes far beyond what you do to make money.

Many people have their day jobs to make ends meet, but they're out on weekends and evenings helping at the food bank or local church youth group.

It's imperative to understand that your job does not define *who you are*. It's only part of *what you do*. Interestingly, when we meet people we often ask them what they *do* to help us figure out what kind of person they are. But to truly understand people, we should ask about their passions and dreams and how they spend their *non-working* hours.

FINDING YOUR VOCATION

There are several practical steps or methods to finding your actual vocation.

Find out what you enjoy. Often you won't know what you like until you force yourself—or someone forces you—to try it. Two somewhat humorous examples of this come thanks to our daughter.

Lorelle was a rather picky eater, and it was painful to get her to try new foods when she was little. One day we offered her chocolate, and she adamantly refused. Being an awful parent, I ran out of patience, grabbed a little piece of chocolate, and pushed it into her mouth. She began to cry, mouth wide open, refusing to eat it. Then suddenly she stopped crying. Her eyes widened as she experienced the delights of chocolate for the very first time! She has loved chocolate ever since.

Another time, when she was about seven or eight years old, we were at Playland, an amusement park in Vancouver. Both kids were finally tall enough to go on the Corkscrew rollercoaster. Leanne and I are big rollercoaster fans, and we were tired of the kiddie rides, so we decided to try to persuade the kids to go on the coaster with us. Lorelle refused, of course, and I did what I thought I would never do: I bribed her. We had a small, second-hand toy at home that we hadn't given her yet, so I offered the deal. Finally, she looked at me grumpily and said, "Fine."

We got in line and waited in tense silence for our turn. Finally we got on the rollercoaster. I sat with Lorelle, and Leanne sat with Ben. As we slowly made our way up the first big hill. Lorelle started wailing in fear. That was when I realized that I was probably the worst father in the history of the world. As the rollercoaster crested the hill and began its descent into breakneck turns and loops, Lorelle fell silent, and I figured she was too distraught even to scream. Finally we slowed down, went around the last couple of corners, and entered the station. I fearfully looked over at Lorelle, wondering if she would stop hating me by the time she was sixteen. She had a surprisingly serene look on her face, almost pleased, like when she first tried chocolate. She looked up at me and said those five most beautiful words: "Daddy, can we go again?" And we did—twice more!

> **BONUS TIP**: Just because you get your desired result doesn't make your methodology right.

From then on, whenever we went to any kind of amusement park, Lorelle was the one pushing us to go on the fastest rollercoaster *just one more time*. Granted, it was probably wrong for me to force my child to eat chocolate or go on a rollercoaster. I thought I knew her well enough to know what she would like, and I was correct in those instances. Ignore my parenting methods for now; the point is that we don't know what we enjoy until we try things. Sometimes you need to embrace the adventure and go for it!

Discover what you're good at. You'll probably excel at many things you've never tried. Guess how you can find out? Yes, go and try!

You might become a fantastic teacher, but you may never know until you try leading a small group or a children's program a few times. I had no idea I would be good at working with kids and youth until I tried it. It was the same with preaching, teaching, and writing. Yet as I did each of those things, I found success, and people I trusted told me they liked what I was doing.

I also tried things I wasn't very good at, like working on a construction site for a few months. Not only did I dislike the work, but I was a hazard to those around me! Once, I was working up in the rafters of a building, and I foolishly put my hammer down on a beam. I bumped it, and it dropped about twenty feet, landing in the sand right behind another worker! He didn't hear or see the hammer that almost clocked him. I quietly made my way down, casually walked behind him, picked up my hammer, and went back up without him even noticing. I never did that again, but it didn't take long to realize that I wasn't cut out for that kind of work. I tried numerous other things I didn't do well at, so I learned and moved on.

> **BONUS TIP:** There are times when failures should make us dig deeper and try harder, but there are also times when failures show us we're on the wrong path. Learn to distinguish between the two.

Generally, your vocation connects to things you're *good at* and things that bring you *joy* and *fulfillment*. Try serving in many different settings, and ask people you trust how they thought you did.

Find your passions. Some people are generally more passionate than others, but we all have things we deeply care about, no matter how we show it. We need to consider carefully what those things are.

If we're honest, we realize that people care most deeply about themselves. Yet as God gets hold of our hearts, and as we get to know Jesus, he changes our desires to areas of his passion. Psalm 37:4 says, *"Delight yourself in the Lord, and he will give you the desires of your heart."* This sounds like a recipe for getting what we most want. The key is in delighting in God. When we genuinely seek him and what he wants in this world, he changes our desires to make them godly desires. What does God desire? Two of his most frequently stated passions are that all people should repent and come to know him (e.g., 2 Peter 3:9) and that those who are least able to help themselves would be looked after, such as widows and orphans (e.g., James 1:27).

If you discover a passion for reaching the lost or helping the disadvantaged, you might already have a God-given vocation. Regardless, learn to tap into your God-given desires to see where he would have you serve.

Understand your spiritual gifting. God gives us different gifts to do his work in the local church and our communities. You can find examples of these in Romans 12, 1 Corinthians 12, 1 Peter 4, and Ephesians 4. None of the lists are the same, which suggests that these aren't exhaustive lists but rather examples to help us understand the types of gifts God's Spirit gives.

You weren't born with your gifts. This sets them apart from natural talents. God equips believers with specific gifts his Church requires to serve him and meet various needs. Some people place a lot of emphasis on taking spiritual gift tests or indicators, and these can be helpful. You can find them online, and they'll indicate the kinds of gifts you may have.

However, the most accurate way to discover your gifts is to get involved with various types of ministry. You will, over time, start to see what areas bring you success and joy. At the same time, consider that sometimes God asks us to work in areas we simply aren't good at so that we learn to depend more on Him.

Recognize your unique personality and experiences. It also helps to recognize that your personality and experiences can lead you to understand what vocation would suit you. For example, people who have been abused can often succeed in a ministry to others who have been abused.

Many aspects of our personalities and experiences may seem to be disadvantages, yet God can use them to reach people in unexpected ways. My passionate nature, which caused me to get into fights as a kid, still gets me in trouble occasionally. However, it has also helped me persevere when things got tough, which has been vital in my current role.

Sometimes the best leaders have been hurt in various ways and can now comfort others who go through similar circumstances. Paul wrote this in 2 Corinthians 1:3–4:

> *Blessed be the … God of all comfort, who comforts us in all our affliction, so that we may be able to comfort those who are in any affliction, with the comfort with which we ourselves are comforted by God.*

Recognize God's calling. God's calling is mysterious. He doesn't call every believer into professional ministry; however, there is a general call for all believers to follow Jesus, take up their crosses daily, and live for him regardless of their work. God has called you to be a full-time Christian, no matter what vocation he has given you. Still, God clearly calls certain people to specific positions and ministries, such as pastoring or missionary work. Often that call is felt in restlessness and a lack of peace until the person obeys him.

I felt God's calling in grade twelve. I went forward in a church service to publicly say, "Yes, Lord, I am willing to serve you wherever you lead me." I felt it again when I went to Hedley and when I came to Timberline. I even felt it when I went to work in that difficult church situation, though it didn't seem to make sense for a while, especially after I left so soon.

Often it's that sense of calling—knowing that God has you where he wants you—that allows you to make it through the tough times. If you're genuinely seeking God, I believe he will, over time, clearly show you where he wants you to serve. It may not have anything to do with how you make money or support your family.

> BONUS TIP: Don't be disappointed if God doesn't call you into full-time Christian ministry. This world needs faithful Christians in various careers, shining the light of Jesus into the darkest corners.

Understand your true ministry. There's a real danger in making this much too complicated, as though we can't serve God until we know exactly what he wants from us. If you ignore everything else in this section, understand this one thing: your ministry is the people around you at any given time. Read that again. Although it's helpful to think about jobs and vocations, what matters most is that we see ministry as *people*, not programs, and not causes. Each of us was created for a great purpose, but it's too easy to focus on discovering that purpose instead of simply seeing the needs around us and responding to them.

I remember watching a cheesy Christian movie back in the early 1980s in which the main character was told by an angel that God had a great purpose for his life. As this went to his head, he had all these grand ideas of how he could serve the Lord. By focusing on that, he missed opportunities to help people around him, particularly one guy who specifically needed his help. In the end, the angel told him that helping the guy he was ignoring was his great purpose, and he had missed it completely! Apparently, even cheesy Christian movies can be impactful, because I have thought about that many times in the subsequent years.

Similarly, we see this in the story Jesus told about the Good Samaritan (Luke 10:25–37). A man is robbed and left for dead at the side of the road. A priest and a Levite, those set apart for God's work, come by. They see him lying there but cross to the other side of the road to avoid going near him. Maybe they had other important work to do and didn't want to be delayed, or perhaps they were afraid to be made ceremonially unclean. Regardless, it's clear that their ministry—what God would have had them do at that moment—was to help the dying man. The story continues to show an enemy of the dying man (a Samaritan) as the only one who understood his ministry. He went far out of his way to help the man, at a high personal cost.

Be aware that God has purpose and meaning for your life, abilities, gifts, passions, and personality. Look at what your true vocation should be, even apart from how you make a living. But also pray that God would help you see the opportunities around you every day and wherever you go.

THE SECRET TO SUCCESS

Everyone wants to be successful in life, but what is success?

When God led his people, the Israelites, into the land he had promised them for generations, they were about to come against fortified cities, trained armies, giant warriors, and seemingly impossible odds. God retired Moses and installed Joshua as Israel's new leader. It was a daunting task, but God had prepared him to succeed. Look at what God told Joshua at the beginning of his new vocation:

> *No man shall be able to stand before you all the days of your life. Just as I was with Moses, so* I will be with you. *I will not leave you or forsake you. Be strong and courageous, for you shall cause this people to inherit the*

*land that I swore to their fathers to give them. Only be
strong and very courageous, being careful to do according
to all the law that Moses my servant commanded you.*
(Joshua 1:5–7a, emphasis added)

Of first importance, Joshua would succeed as he trusted God's
presence in his life. He could be courageous and strong, knowing that
God went with him. And then God tells Joshua that to be successful, he
must stay on the path God had given him, obeying God's Word. Sound
familiar?

*Do not turn from it to the right hand or to the left, that
you may have good success wherever you go. This Book
of the Law shall not depart from your mouth, but you
shall meditate on it day and night, so that you may be
careful to do according to all that is written in it. For
then you will make your way prosperous, and then you
will have good success. Have I not commanded you? Be
strong and courageous. Do not be frightened, and do not
be dismayed, for the Lord your God is with you wherever
you go."* (Joshua 1:7b–9)

Success has two aspects: *trust* and *obedience*. It sounds so simple, and
it is. Not easy, but simple. God says, "I am going with you. I have given
you my laws. Now meditate on my will for you, day and night, be sure
to obey me, and then I will make you successful."

EARLY MISSIONARIES

Many early Christian missionaries in places like Africa toiled for
decades and rarely saw even a single person come to Christ. Does
that mean they were unsuccessful? By the world's standards, they were
not only unsuccessful, but they were foolish to waste their lives on
such things. Yet they trusted God and obeyed him. Incredibly, the
following generation of missionaries who obeyed God's call to go to
these countries found the people ready to receive the gospel gladly.

Hundreds of thousands were saved in a few short years! Were those later missionaries more successful than those who died without seeing many people believe? Was their success based on the number of people saved or their obedience to God?

In 1893, a Canadian named Walter Gowan envisioned reaching the sixty million Africans of north-central Africa with the gospel. He took two men with him, Rowland Bingham and Thomas Kent. It was seemingly a disaster from the start. Walter was captured by slave raiders and eventually managed to get free, but he died of malaria in Africa. The other two also got very sick, and Thomas also died while still in Africa. Only Rowland Bingham made it home again.

After Rowland recovered, he returned to Africa but failed in a second attempt to establish a mission. However, in 1903—on his third attempt—he finally established a base in Nigeria. This was the beginning of what came to be known as the "Sudan Interior Mission," which soon reached tens of thousands of souls for Jesus! Today, over four thousand SIM missionaries serve in more than seventy countries worldwide.

When Rowland went home after losing his two friends in Africa, he took Walter's few belongings to Walter's mother. Mrs. Gowan met Roland with an extended hand. Rowland recalls:

> We stood there in silence. Then she said these words: "Well, Mr. Bingham, I would rather have had Walter go out to the Sudan and die there, all alone, than have him home today, disobeying his Lord."[8]

These words have challenged me for years. Could I have that attitude if I lost one of my children like that? Could I serve God in such a place, knowing that I could so easily die? Despite Mrs. Gowan's sorrow at losing her son, she was willing to put God's purposes ahead of her own. She recognized success—not failure—in her son's obedience.

BONUS TIP: It's much better to die young while faithfully serving God than to live a long life of mediocrity.

Another famous missionary, Jim Elliot, was savagely murdered alongside four other missionaries while serving Jesus in Ecuador. He was only twenty-nine and left behind a wife and daughter. They eventually went and lived among the natives who had killed Jim, and they saw many come to trust in Christ. Before Jim died, he wrote, "He is no fool who gives what he cannot keep to gain what he cannot lose."[9]

Jim knew the dangers but chose the path of obedience. Similarly, the great missionary Hudson Taylor died in China after a lifetime of serving his Lord and losing both his wife and children there. Earlier, he wrote, "If I had one thousand lives, I'd give them all for China."[10] How can we help but look at their lives and acknowledge that they were amazingly successful in God's eyes? Success is found in living for God, trusting and obeying him, no matter what happens. It's not based on whether God allows us to see the fruit of our hard work. The reward is Christ's presence in this life and in eternity.

God made us to live in a joyful relationship with him and bring glory to him, but so often we settle for the accolades of people. I may not understand why things happen the way they do, but I want all my life to be dedicated to his will and glory.

THE GREAT ADVENTURE

God wants so much more for you than you can even comprehend. Throughout this book, we've discussed how to choose the right path and stay on that path. However, there is never a guarantee that the way will be easy or that it will be clear for miles ahead. Once you choose to follow Jesus on his paths of life, it may often *feel* unsafe, but you will never be bored!

I read a poem once about the Christian life being somewhat like a tandem bicycle.[11] At first, we trust Jesus for salvation, and we figuratively put him in the back seat so we can continue to steer. Our paths are safe and predictable, but we know something is missing. However, when we finally give up control, Jesus takes the front seat, and then life truly begins! He takes us around curves and corners at speeds that frighten us, over rocks and roots and jumps, along daring shortcuts and unexpected views and vistas. At times we may complain that we don't know where we're going, but he just laughs, looks back, and tells us to keep pedaling.

Jesus didn't leave the glory of heaven, suffer, and die for us so that we could live comfortable, middle-class lives with a nice house and perfect children. Jesus said, *"I came that they may have life and have it abundantly"* (John 10:10b). Abundant *life!* Not just survival, not just getting by and following a predictable path, but *life!*

> **BONUS TIP:** If you think living for Jesus is boring, you're probably doing it wrong!

Sometimes we need to just get on the rollercoaster without being bribed. Sometimes we need to allow God to give us chocolate without forcing it into our mouths. Then we realize that he's offering us something wonderful. Yet we resist and seemingly want baby food for the rest of our lives. He offers us true adventure, but we settle for movies, video games, and coffee. He wants to truly satisfy us with water from his clean, pure well, but we're content with oily water from a puddle on the road.

We are made for a relationship with God, so nothing else will satisfy us. To embrace the adventure he offers us is to embrace the calling he has put on our lives to follow him in every circumstance. And boy, is it worthwhile!

CHOOSE YOUR OWN ADVENTURE

The Wise Path: I choose to give my life to following and serving Jesus, no matter where he leads me, recognizing that every interaction with a person is an opportunity to shine his light.

The Foolish Path: I choose to live each day for myself, ignoring the opportunities God has given me to make a meaningful difference in this world.

— Chapter Ten —
HEADING FOR HOME

Thus says the Lord:
Stand by the roads, and look, and ask for the ancient paths,
where the good way is; and walk in it,
and find rest for your souls.
~ Jeremiah 6:16a

There's nothing quite like heading out on a new trail, full of energy and anticipation, the day ahead of you, enjoying companionship. I love that feeling, especially when there's still a bit of a chill in the air, some dampness from the night before, and everything smells so fresh and new.

Fast forward several hours later to when I'm on the trail heading back, and there often comes a time when I'm just ready to go home. Usually this is because it's been a great day and I feel satisfied with all that was seen and done, but sometimes it's because the weather turned nasty, someone got injured, or something else went wrong. Or it might even be a mixture of good and bad experiences—I'm just done!

This may be similar for Christians as we approach the end of our lives. If we've stayed on the path and served Jesus faithfully, we can hardly wait to go home to be with our heavenly Father. There's the satisfaction in a well-lived life and the anticipation of the end of hardships.

A few years ago, on my birthday, Leanne and I were hiking in Golden Ears Park. On the way back, I was looking for a trail after getting a little off-course, and I slipped through a rotten log, injuring my lower leg. We were close to an hour from the car, and as my leg swelled, it became very painful to walk. We managed to find the trail—I knew it was there!—but wow, was that a difficult hobble back. I was so glad to get to the parking lot, drive home, and get some ice on my leg. Still, it was a great day, and I was glad we went—even when my leg turned purple a day or two later!

Unlike a hiking trail that leads back to where we started, the trail of life moves ever onward with no discernible ending point. We simply don't know when we'll come around a bend and find ourselves at the gates of heaven. The big question is: Am I ready for that day?

Suddenly, one day, we will come face to face with God. Somehow, I have always felt like there should be some kind of warning, but the fact is, I could die instantly in a car accident or from a heart attack—even before I finish writing this chapter. So I'd better keep going!

How can we make sure we're ready for that day? That's the subject of this final chapter.

DARE TO RISK

Do you ever wish that you had courage like other people you know? We see someone stand up to speak, sing, or perform in front of their peers, and we marvel at their bravery. "They're so fearless!"

When interning as a pastor at Central Baptist Church in Victoria, I asked the senior pastor if he ever got nervous preaching after twenty-plus years. His answer surprised me. "Every time," he said. He sure had me fooled! But I certainly felt better about my nervousness as I prepared to preach.

Courage is not a lack of fear. It's being afraid or nervous and *doing it anyway*. If you're not afraid, no courage is required. Fear doesn't have to immobilize us. Oxford defines courage as "the ability to do something that frightens one" or "strength in the face of pain or grief."[12]

When attempting something that intimidates me, I often ask myself two questions:

1. What is the worst thing that could happen if I do this?
2. What will I miss out on if I don't do this?

These are the questions of "risk versus reward." For example, you should consider the *risk* of going onto a high cliff ledge to get a good view or take a photo. Is there a chance you could slip and be killed or badly injured? Then consider the *reward*: what kind of view or photo might you get? If there's a high risk of injury, the reward of the view may not be worthwhile. But if there's a protective fence or a safe place to stand, that much smaller risk is probably worth the reward.

In public speaking, the risk is that you could speak badly, forget what you planned to say, or say something ridiculous (I have done all of these). Those things could lead to embarrassment. But is that so terrible? As we discussed earlier, failure is often good for us, providing opportunities for growth and development. "But what if people think I'm a bad speaker?" So what? Maybe you are. You might just need some practice. Repeated failure may also show you that public speaking isn't something you should pursue.

The reward (or loss of reward) is equally essential to consider. If you do *not* take this opportunity, you may miss out on an opportunity for personal growth. Or you might lose a chance to share your passions or something you have learned that will help someone else. If you're convinced that God has called you to speak, you risk disobeying if you cop out. You can miss so much if you don't take the opportunities given. It can be helpful to ask yourself: Which is the more considerable risk, failure or stagnancy? As someone suggested, you can play it safe all your life and still slip in the bathtub and break your neck—and it will serve you right!

Risk and reward. If we're living full-out for Jesus, obeying his leading, what's the risk? The worst that can happen is that we die (and gain heaven!), which can't happen until God allows it, so what are we afraid of? Truly no danger can touch us apart from God's allowance for his greater purposes.

This doesn't remove our responsibility to live wisely. I've often considered a scenario where I do something stupid, like ignoring a DANGER sign on a fence, and then fall to my death. I get to heaven and complain, "God! You didn't protect me!" And he says, "Of course I protected you! I put that sign there, gave you eyes to read and a brain to choose wisely, but you ignored all that! What more did you want me to do?" Still, the wisest thing isn't always what feels safest, either.

My father built a sailboat—in our front yard—as I was growing up. Once when we were out sailing, a thunderstorm suddenly blew up. The wind grew strong, the waves got big, and I could tell my parents were worried about the big steel mast being struck by lightning. I was afraid, but I trusted that my dad knew what to do. He immediately lowered the sail, put the family safely below, and used the little motor to take us quickly back to safety. I was afraid, but my father knew what to do, and I knew I could trust him.

This reminds me of when the disciples were crossing the Sea of Galilee:

> *And a great windstorm arose, and the waves were breaking into the boat, so that the boat was already filling. But he was in the stern, asleep on the cushion. And they woke him and said to him, "Teacher, do you not care that we are perishing?" And he awoke and rebuked the wind and said to the sea, "Peace! Be still!" And the wind ceased, and there was a great calm. He said to them, "Why are you so afraid? Have you still no faith?" And they were filled with great fear and said to one another, "Who then is this, that even the wind and the sea obey him?"* (Mark 4:37–41)

I love that! Jesus was right there, and they asked him, "Don't you care?" So he calmed the sea with a word, and there was immediate peace. They just needed to trust him. Yet it's interesting: the winds died down, and *then* it says, *"And they were filled with great fear."* Jesus didn't remove their fear; he redirected it to the right place—him.

When we understand God's power, we learn to fear *only him*, knowing he holds our eternal destiny in his hands. But in fearing him, we discover that there is nothing else in the world to fear! And because we are his children and loved by him, that fear never has to paralyze us. Instead, it leads to a deep reverence for him.

"WHAT IF" VERSUS "EVEN IF"

You may be familiar with the story in Daniel 3 of the three young men who were captured, taken to Babylon, and later expected to bow down to a giant idol. When they refused, they were given one last chance before being executed. I love their response:

> ... *our God whom we serve is able to deliver us from the burning fiery furnace, and he will deliver us out of your hand, O king. But if not, be it known to you, O king, that we will not serve your gods or worship the golden image that you have set up.* (Daniel 3:17–18)

They believed God could and would save them. But *even if* he chose not to, they would bravely face the literal fiery furnace of the king's wrath. Why? Because they knew that it was wrong to bow to an idol. Because they feared God more than the king. Because their faith in God and fear of God surpassed their fear of any man or circumstance.

There is such a difference between a "what if" attitude and an "even if" attitude. The disciples saw the wind and thought, "*What if* we sink?" If they had known and trusted Jesus more, they would have thought, "*Even if* we sink, Jesus is here with us. It will be okay!"

> BONUS TIP: Although it will often *feel* dangerous, there's never a genuine risk in following Jesus. We need to acknowledge that when things are beyond our control (and they usually are), they are never beyond *his* control.

When I first learned to rock climb, I remember the sheer terror of being high off the ground, dangling from a precipice. It felt like one mistake would send me dropping to my death! Sure, I wore a helmet and a harness, and a strong rope was attached to me. But what if it failed? What if it couldn't hold me when I fell? I had to learn to trust that the rope was constructed to hold more than thirty times my weight! It could hold a mid-size SUV, so surely it could hold me.

Similarly, when we consider the *power* of God and the *promises* of God to sustain us, the risk of putting our full trust in him is imaginary.

People often say, "God will never give you anything you can't handle." That's a lie from the devil! Of course God will give you more than you can handle—so that you'll depend on him and not on yourself. A more trustworthy saying would be, "God will never give you more than *he* can handle." Even when we feel like we're dangling from a cliff, he's got this thing!

What holds you back from the opportunity to step out and do something potentially amazing? Are you thinking, *What if I fail?* Guess what? *Even if* you fail, Jesus is with you, and it will be okay! *Even if* everyone else abandons you, he will stay with you. *Even if* you obey God to the point of martyrdom or death, his reward will be more than you can ever imagine.

Choose your risks well, but do not fear them. We have victory in Jesus Christ!

KEEP THE MAIN THING THE MAIN THING

In light of eternity, what's the most important thing you can do with your time? In chapter nine, we looked at what it means to have a mission in life, to live with purpose. The potential danger with that idea is finding ourselves living for *causes* instead of *Christ*.

When I was in college, we would sometimes have "school spirit days." One time we were starting a new discipleship event called "Grassroots," and we were all supposed to come to chapel wearing green. Of course, that meant my buddy and I were undoubtedly going to be wearing blue! We took it even further, making large posters decrying the evilness of green and the holiness of blue, using well-misplaced verses to support our supposed ideology.

We arrived early, receiving various responses such as laughter, pointing, and even a few uptight individuals who were righteously angry at our supposed misuse of scripture. Why are there always those people? Yet my favorite moment was when a whole hall of girls waltzed in—dressed to the nines in blue! When they saw us, we were suddenly immensely popular with the ladies! It was glorious! It was amazing! It was temporary.

The danger with *causes* is that people tend to get all worked up about something, care about it for a month or two, and then move on to something else. I'm not saying that causes are never worth our time, and I fully support the right to peaceful, law-abiding protest. But we also need to be careful where we put our time and energy.

As I mentioned earlier, one of my heroes is William Wilberforce. He led a movement, over most of his lifetime, to abolish the slave trade in England. He experienced many setbacks and health problems and was often mocked and even humiliated. Many hated and abused him, yet he stuck it through and achieved one of the most significant and unlikely victories in the British parliament imaginable. It took almost fifty years devoted to the cause—and God's hand in it all—to achieve this.

When we look at a man like Wilberforce, we see someone who had a high calling on his life from God. He knew God's will for him and pursued it with everything he had. It wasn't something he joined because it was popular or politically correct. In fact, he went completely *against* the flow of his culture and paid the price for it day after day and year after year. I have nothing but respect for a man like that. If God puts a worthwhile cause upon your heart, you should pursue it passionately.

The trouble is that many of us have strong opinions about things and can tend to see them as very black-and-white. Or blue and green if you prefer. Yet we often lack the fortitude and patience to think things through, work out a sustainable plan, and stick with it for the long term.

> **BONUS TIP:** Most things in life are not black and white. There are significant nuances to almost every issue. Learn to be patient and take the time needed to understand things before forming a strong opinion or taking a side.

There are two important principles to understand. First, we've each been given only a certain amount of time and energy. Whatever you put time and effort into is also a choice *not* to do other things. By spending your time on a *good* thing, you may be choosing not to do something that would be a better use of your time. Sometimes *good* can get in the way of what is *best*.

Consider carefully if your cause is what God wants you to put your time and effort into. For example, is it more vital for you to save the planet than to save those who haven't heard about Jesus and are heading for a godless eternity? You *may* be called to the worthy cause of environmentalism, but you *are* called to make disciples.

Second, remember that there are many sides to any issue. For example, it has always seemed evident that electric cars are better for the environment than gas cars. However, I've recently wondered if it's so simple, especially as I've learned about the mining processes used to produce the batteries. Even the electricity for these cars may not be attained in environmentally friendly ways. It seems we're moving in the right direction with electric cars, but it's not as simple as it once appeared.

Similarly, one might support the concept that cities should have only mass transit and allow no other vehicles within certain limits. Yet we must consider the movement of goods, the costs of such a transition, etc. We should research issues carefully before supporting them.

> BONUS TIP: Research doesn't mean spending twenty minutes looking up articles on the internet.

Christians should undoubtedly be concerned about the environment and carefully steward God's earth. My concern, however, arises when any issue overshadows our primary role as God's ambassadors and witnesses to this world.

If we've been saved through faith in Jesus, the goal of our lives is to put God *first* in everything we do. Not only do we live and worship for an Audience of One, but we make all our choices based on what we believe he would have us do. We need to live for Christ and not expend all our energy on causes unless they are also for the cause of Christ.

So ask yourself: Is this cause truly where God wants me to spend my limited time? Where can I best invest my time to advance his kingdom— not my personal agenda—today?

Never settle for second best. Keep Jesus the main thing in your life.

LIVE BY THE SPIRIT

Years ago, I volunteered with a church youth group that invited me to take a leadership role on a mission trip to Tijuana, Mexico. Working with a local church, we had a women's ministry, a children's ministry, and a sports ministry, which I led.

Our group's task was simple: we took a soccer ball down to a field and soon had many kids playing with us. After an hour or so, we would take a break, share a testimony through an interpreter, and then go back to playing. We also invited them to join us in watching the *Jesus Film* on Thursday night.

I found it humorous that these kids always wanted to play *against* us ("Beat the Gringos!"). Each day, their team included older players to try to beat us. By day four, only men were playing against us, and all the kids were watching! While not entirely ideal—we wanted to play with the kids!—it meant more people we could share Jesus with.

A big crowd gathered outside the church for the film on Thursday evening, and we were excited. I would be giving the gospel presentation and invitation at the end, and I was quite nervous. But that just caused me to pray more desperately that God would work in the hearts of these people—and keep me from screwing up. However, when it came time to watch the film, the projector simply wouldn't work. We tried everything we could—including praying over it—yet nothing. So we scrambled together an alternate program of singing and testimonies and asked everyone to come back the next day, our last in Mexico.

That evening, Dave, a relatively new Christian on my sports ministry team, was extremely upset. "How could God let this happen? What if people don't come back tomorrow? We prayed, and God didn't answer!" I tried to explain that God knows best and that we have to trust him, but it seemed like Dave was ready to give up on God altogether.

> BONUS TIP: One mark of spiritual maturity is learning that God often doesn't let us in on his plans. Instead, he asks us to trust him and wait upon him for his perfect timing.

The next day, we played soccer one last time, and there were some new men out whom we invited to the film that night. Some of them surprisingly came, and the crowd was even bigger than the previous evening. We had a different film projector, and we had tested it ahead of time, so it was all systems go. Except that this one didn't work either!

This was our last chance, and we became desperate. So again we prayed over the projector, pleaded with God for help, and then suddenly, it worked! We all watched the film, I presented the gospel, and then over twenty people came forward to receive Christ as their Lord and Savior!

Although men in Mexico are often very opposed or apathetic to religion, at least two men were saved that night. Amazingly, both had been absent the previous evening. One we had met at soccer for the first time that day; the other just happened to be passing through the neighborhood and came to see what was happening.

When I spoke with Dave afterward, he was so excited! He suddenly saw that God had a purpose, knew what he was doing, and could be trusted. We can't know or orchestrate what God will accomplish through us (and aside from us), but we can obey, pray, and trust in every circumstance.

Living by the Spirit means we regularly take time to wait upon the Lord, listen to his guidance, and move forward in confidence that he will accomplish his purposes. We can start each day by asking him to lead us to people who need to be encouraged, helped, or told about him. We can *"pray without ceasing"* (1 Thessalonians 5:17) throughout the day, submitting to his plans and ways instead of our own.

When we live by the Spirit, he keeps us on the right path, reminds us that we are God's children, strengthens us, helps us know what to pray, and empowers us to live fruitful lives.

> *But I say, walk by the Spirit, and you will not gratify the desires of the flesh.* (Galatians 5:16)

> *For all who are led by the Spirit of God are sons of God.* (Romans 8:14)

> *Likewise the Spirit helps us in our weakness. For we do not know what to pray for as we ought, but the Spirit himself intercedes for us with groanings too deep for words.* (Romans 8:26)

> *But the fruit of the Spirit is love, joy, peace, patience, kindness, goodness, faithfulness, gentleness, self-control; against such things there is no law.* (Galatians 5:22–23)

STAY FUTURE-FOCUSED

The remarkable story of Abraham is found in Genesis 11–25. God chose him to be the father of his Chosen People, Israel, but Abraham still had to choose to obey God. For the most part, Abraham got it right, though not without a few slip-ups (read the story—it's great!). God called him—at seventy-five years old—to leave his homeland and all his relatives and travel hundreds of miles to a land he knew little about (Genesis 12:1).

Abraham obeyed, and God blessed him with a family in his old age. He also provided a covenant promising that Abraham's descendants would someday inherit the land and outnumber the (visible) stars. That was fulfilled over six hundred years later when about two million of his descendants conquered the Promised Land under Joshua.

It must have been incredibly difficult to leave all his relatives behind to obey God this way. About two thousand years later, the writer of Hebrews used his life to demonstrate faithful living:

> *By faith Abraham, when called to go to a place he would later receive as his inheritance, obeyed and went, even though he did not know where he was going. By faith he made his home in the promised land like a stranger in a foreign country; he lived in tents, as did Isaac and Jacob, who were heirs with him of the same promise. For he was looking forward to the city with foundations, whose architect and builder is God.* (Hebrews 11:8–10, NIV)

He could obey, leave everything behind, and live as a nomad without a proper home because *"he was looking forward to the city with foundations, whose architect and builder is God."* In other words, he could look beyond this life and focus on the future kingdom of God, where God would provide him a much better home—built upon the foundation of Jesus Christ—than he could ever wish for in this lifetime. What great faith!

> **BONUS TIP:** Having faith isn't knowing the route or details of the destination. It's knowing the one who is taking you there and believing he is *good*.

I must constantly remind myself that this life is only the tiniest of beginnings. If I live here even eighty or ninety years, it's almost nothing in view of eternity. So I don't need a mansion here, riches, fame, or anything that would keep my heart tied to this place. My real home is the new heaven and the new earth, which may be just around the bend! My future is secured and glorious, so I need to keep my eyes on the finish line. As Paul wrote towards the end of his life: *"But one thing I do: forgetting what lies behind and straining forward to what lies ahead, I press on toward the goal for the prize of the upward call of God in Christ Jesus"* (Philippians 3:13b–14).

OUR FINAL DESTINATION

So often when I sing a song about the return of the Lord, my eyes well up with tears and I begin to choke up because my heart's greatest desire is to be with Christ, to go to my true home. More than anything, I look forward to that day when Christ returns. He will remake this world and bring everlasting peace and joy.

Most people believe that we can never predict the future. While this is true in specific details, the big picture of coming events has been laid out very clearly in the Word of God. Consider three—of many— passages about the future of humanity:

For the Lord himself will descend from heaven with a cry of command, with the voice of an archangel, and with the sound of the trumpet of God. And the dead in Christ will rise first. Then we who are alive, who are left, will be caught up together with them in the clouds to meet the Lord in the air, and so we will always be with the Lord. Therefore encourage one another with these words. (1 Thessalonians 4:16–18)

Then I saw a great white throne and him who was seated on it. From his presence earth and sky fled away, and no place was found for them. And I saw the dead, great and small, standing before the throne, and books were opened. Then another book was opened, which is the book of life. And the dead were judged by what was written in the books, according to what they had done ... And if anyone's name was not found written in the book of life, he was thrown into the lake of fire. (Revelation 20:11–12, 15)

Then I saw a new heaven and a new earth, for the first heaven and the first earth had passed away, and the sea was no more. And I saw the holy city, new Jerusalem, coming down out of heaven from God, prepared as a bride adorned for her husband. And I heard a loud voice from the throne saying, "Behold, the dwelling place of God is with man. He will dwell with them, and they will be his people, and God himself will be with them as their God. He will wipe away every tear from their eyes, and death shall be no more, neither shall there be mourning, nor crying, nor pain anymore, for the former things have passed away." (Revelation 21:1–4)

We could summarize these three passages with two words: Jesus wins! The great news is that if we are in Christ—saved by his sacrifice—we win too!

The big picture is very clear in God's Word. If you live for yourself, you will gain pleasure now and sorrow for eternity. But if you live for Jesus, you may be sorrowful now, but you will gain ultimate pleasure in the world to come.

THE END OF THE ROAD

I will conclude with one final story. In high school, I drove a "beater," a 1967 Vauxhall Viva. We called it Albie (i.e., "LB" or "Little Beast"). It was old, even in 1985. It was so gutless that it would take about twenty seconds on a flat highway to get from fifty to seventy-five kilometers an hour, and then it would start to shake horrendously!

I was working at a McDonald's about twenty minutes away from home, and I knew my gas tank was low, but I wasn't sure how low because the gauge wasn't exact. I only had five dollars in my wallet and no credit or bank card, and I wanted to get my paycheck from work before filling up so that I wouldn't have to go to the gas station twice. I was smart that way.

Sure enough, about halfway to work—after ignoring several gas stations along the way—Albie ran out of gas. One second I had power; the next, I was coasting along a busy street, trying to find a safe place to pull over. I was quite far from a gas station by this time, so I went to a nearby house and asked if someone could drive me. They surprisingly agreed to, and the gas station was kind enough to lend me a gas container to fill with my five dollars of gas. Then I got a ride back to my car, put the gas in the car, and drove back to the gas station to drop off the container. All because I was too lazy to go get gas twice.

Our lives are like cars with no gas gauge and no spare gas. We have no idea how much farther we can go. We don't know whether we have eighty years left (okay, I know I don't!), fifty years to go (still unlikely), twenty years left, or just five minutes.

Someday, likely without warning, my heart will stop beating, and I'll arrive instantly at my final destination. At that point, it won't matter what kind of car I had or how it looked. The only question remaining will be: Where did I take that car while it still had gas in the tank? Which roads did I drive along? Whom did I bring along for the ride?

Did I pick anyone up and drive them to the gas station? What did I do with the time and distance God gave me? We all choose our route, and at some unknown time in the near or far future, we will arrive.

And that's it.

I pray that you will take the path—the road—that leads to eternal life and use every hour of every day to serve the King. One last time, Jesus said,

> *Enter by the narrow gate. For the gate is wide and the way is easy that leads to destruction, and those who enter by it are many. For the gate is narrow and the way is hard that leads to life, and those who find it are few.* (Matthew 7:13–14)

In the end, there were only ever two paths to choose from. Which one are you on? Do you know where it's taking you?

I am so grateful to know where I'm going. I don't know all the paths Jesus is going to take me along, but I know where he's taking me, and it's going to be amazing!

I hope and pray that we can meet on the other side when that day comes. In the meantime, let's live wisely, stay on track, and glorify our King. Come, Lord Jesus!

CHOOSE YOUR OWN ADVENTURE

The Wise Path: I choose to focus on the prize at the end instead of the difficulties along the way, trusting God's Spirit to guide me along the best paths.

The Foolish Path: I choose to live for today and ignore that nagging feeling from God's Spirit that I am headed for destruction.

Endnotes

1. "Ralph Waldo Emerson Quotes," Goodreads, accessed May 5, 2023, https://www. goodreads.com/author/quotes/12080.Ralph_Waldo_Emerson?page=4.
2. "A.W. Tozer Quotes," Goodreads, accessed May 5, 2023, https://www.goodreads. com/quotes/159298-what-comes-into-our-minds-when-we-think-about-god.
3. Believing in consequences is not the same as Karma. Karma is based on cycles of birth and rebirth, which is much different than the "sowing and reaping" principle taught in the Bible.
4. BrainyQuote, accessed May 6, 2023, https://www.brainyquote.com/quotes/albert_ einstein_109012.
5. BrainyQuote, accessed May 6, 2023, https://www.brainyquote.com/quotes/ thomas_a_edison_132683.
6. "Oswald Chambers Quotes,: Goodreads, accessed May 7, 2023, https://www. goodreads.com/quotes/749592-worship-is-giving-god-the-best-that-he-has-given.
7. "'God Made Me Fast and When I Run, I Feel His Pleasure' Do You?" HillFaith, accessed May 7, 2023, https://www.hillfaith.org/apologetics/god-made-me-fast- and-when-i-run-i-feel-his-pleasure/.
8. Dan Graves, "Walter Gowan's Life Drained out for Sudan," Christianity.com, May 3, 2010, https://www.christianity.com/church/church-history/timeline/1801-1900/ walter-gowans-life-drained-out-for-sudan-11630546.html.
9. Jim Elliot Quotes, Goodreads, accessed May 19, 2023, https://www.goodreads.com/ quotes/1053519-he-is-no-fool-who-gives-what-he-cannot-keep.
10. Quotefancy, accessed May 7, 2023, https://quotefancy.com/quote/1491441/James- Hudson-Taylor-If-I-had-1-000-lives-I-d-give-them-all-for-China.
11. Tim Hansel, "The Road of Life (a poem about Jesus riding a tandem bicycle)," Chris Teien, accessed May 19, 2023, https://christeien.com/2020/05/15/the-road- of-life/.
12. Mary Bradley, "How Everyday Life Demands Our Courage," GoodTherapy, March 9, 2016, accessed May 24, 2023, https://www.goodtherapy.org/blog/everyday-life- demands-courage-03098164.

www.ingramcontent.com/pod-product-compliance
Lightning Source LLC
Chambersburg PA
CBHW021059090426
42738CB00006B/418